MERGERS

A EUROPEAN APPROACH TO TECHNIQUE

N. R. A. KREKEL
T. G. VAN DER WOERD
J. J. WOUTERSE

English Edition Edited by
Margaret Allen

Business Books Limited · London

First published in Dutch in 1967 as
Ontwikkeling Samenwerking Fusie
by N. Samsom N.V.

English Language Edition first published in 1969
by Business Books Limited

© KREKEL—VAN DER WOERD—WOUTERSE ASS. 1967 and 1969

S B N 220 66871 X
This book has been set in 10 on 12 pt Baskerville 169
printed in England at the Pitman Press, Bath
for the publishers, Business Books Ltd (Registered Office:
180 Fleet Street, London E.C.4),
publishing offices: Mercury House, Waterloo Road, London S.E.1

MADE AND PRINTED IN GREAT BRITAIN

MERGERS

A EUROPEAN APPROACH TO TECHNIQUE

Contents

Illustrations

1 Introduction

This book is based on a series of articles dealing with company development, co-operation and mergers, but it also contains a working plan for a merger which has not previously been published. This plan can be taken as an illustration of how a merger works out in practice, but it can also be used as a general working guide by the partners in any merger.

The object has been to assemble the ideas which have been developed from several years' practical experience in the rather specialized field of management consultancy and mergers. The original articles have been linked together and placed in a specific context, but they may still be read in any sequence, as each chapter deals with a specific aspect of the subject.

Had we set the articles out in chronological order they would show a perceptible development. However, opinions and ideas were gradually evolved which can be applied to the study of the future prospects of any firm. For the book, a sequence on this basis seemed more important than chronological development. Nevertheless, we feel that an explanation of chronological development is due to readers.

The first article to be published was 'Calculated merging', which here appears in section 4. In this we gave an example of how one aspect of the problem of merging could be tackled with the help of the organization, methods and techniques then known. It was worked out on punched-card equipment and clearly reflects the methods, attitude and mentality of the O & M consultant.

It is less easy to recognize the organization consultant in two more recent reports, 'The problem of succession' and 'The network plan for a merger', which discuss problems and aspects of management which the O & M consultant does not usually deal with. In trying to explain these changes, we concluded that helping to solve problems which concern the entire enterprise (continuity, development, co-operation), but which occur only intermittently or even only once in the lifetime of a firm (succession, merger), makes very special demands on the person involved in those problems.

These demands arise partly from the once-for-all and incidental nature of the problems; from the fact that at such times a comparatively large number of very different experts are required to solve the same problem; and because at such moments unbusinesslike arguments, emotional considerations, etc., often play a part and confuse the issue.

Such experts as the solicitor, lawyer, financial expert, actuary, auditor, valuer and O & M consultant all contribute to the operation. There is, however, no specialization which concerns itself with welding together the contributions from each specialist into a logical and integrated whole.

Success in such an operation requires adaptation to the special demands made by the job. It involves the following:

(a) Putting oneself in the place of the management when considering the objectives of the enterprise, analysing the possibility of realizing their purposes in harmony with society generally, and helping to shape these areas into a clear plan for the firm's development.

(b) Obtaining sufficient knowledge of the various specialized fields and building up such contacts with the experts who must be consulted, so that in discussions and in the final design, justice can be done to every aspect of the management's aims.

(c) In some cases (and always with the full approval of the principals) it means stepping outside the role of adviser and directly representing the interests of the clients in complicated negotiations between the parties, or with companies, financiers, or possible suppliers, buyers, etc.

(d) In a limited number of cases (and again with the express approval of those concerned) it may require taking part in the management of the firm at critical stages in its development, or providing security for any capital raised for the firm. Participation in the management of the firm may also be necessary when dealing with problems of succession. As a rule, however, this participation is limited to the financial-economic aspects of management.

We must stress that these demands arose in practice as essential requirements in the existing situation and were not part of our original intention. They were simply consequences of our—consciously chosen—specialization.

This raises the question of what special needs are required to assist the businessman at the present time. Our dynamic society, with its technical and economic developments, increasing internationalization, etc., is causing drastic changes, or perhaps we should say accelerated changes. EEC, EFTA, automation, concentration, large-scale industry and mass consumption are all symptoms of these changes. For the businessman the point is to ensure the continuity of his firm as society changes. Continuity concerns the enterprise as a whole, and increasingly this kind of problem is arising in the life of every firm. The aspect of efficiency in management—a favourite theme since the Second World War—is gradually yielding its dominant place.

Thinking along these lines, we believe that anyone will arrive at conclusions similar to those which we have been taught by experience.

CONCEPTS OF DEVELOPMENT, CO-OPERATION, MERGER AND TAKE-OVER

There is a great deal of confusion all over the world regarding the concepts of development, co-operation and merger. As a result, the emotional content of some of these concepts has increased, but at the same time the correct usage and understanding of the terms has steadily diminished.

DEVELOPMENT

This is certainly true of the term *company development*. Whereas on the one hand a great number of businesses—mainly the smaller and medium-sized ones—hardly use the concept or may not even know it, there are also firms (chiefly the larger ones) which give the impression that they use the words 'company development' as synonymous with growth, and nothing more. Other (mainly American) firms seem to think that the term 'company development' is identical with 'dealing in firms' and give the impression that the potential earning capacity of a firm is the one and only reason for a take-over. The American 'acquisition' fits into this category and is somewhat comparable with decorating a Christmas tree and hanging on anything which glitters.

Certainly a great number of firms with over 5,000 employees, and almost all the very large firms (over 20,000 employees) have separate departments concerned with long-term development. 'Business Acquisition', 'Corporate Planning' and 'Company Development' are some of the names they are given. These departments have—and are constantly modifying—a long-term development plan for their company as a whole.

The structure of the company and its further development are considered against the background of the structure and development of the section of industry or society with which they are concerned, and an effort is made to make both developments run parallel—in other words, to integrate the development of the company with that of society.

This may mean that plans are made for a directed growth, perhaps an 'acquisition for growth'. It may also mean that plans are made to alter the structure of the firm or to consolidate a development.

The moment and the method of entry into a new market, a new sector of industry, a new country or continent are planned. The strong and the weak points of the company are assessed and ways of development are sought which will strengthen the balanced structure of the firm, either alone or by co-operation, take-overs, mergers and suchlike. It is becoming more and more important for the smaller and medium-sized firm to find the right answer to these problems, as the dangers threatening their continuity are steadily increasing.

Another reason for the attention we have paid to planned development is our conviction that all forms of co-operation between firms should be part of, or preceded by, a company development plan. In practice this is often not the case.

CO-OPERATION

A consequence and result of the company development plan may be co-operation in some form or another with other firms. Probably the confusion surrounding the term 'co-operation' is even greater than that concerning 'development'. Many people appear to regard co-operating as identical with merging; still others think any kind of amalgamation is a merger. An added danger of this confusion is that the purpose or the aims of co-operation are sometimes made subordinate to the choice of the form and direction of the co-operation.

This is the main reason for laying such stress on the purpose of co-operation. Its purpose should always be to strengthen one or more of the basic functions of business—trade, production and development—with regard both to products and production methods. In so doing, it is not enough to know that one is aiming at; for instance, a lowering of the costs, a strengthening of the market position, the development of a dominant position and the improvement of research and development. One should also know how and by what means these purposes can be realized. Once one knows exactly what one wishes to achieve, everything that follows can be made subordinate to this aim. In some cases it may even mean that the particular agreement one had in mind proves meaningless and must be rejected, or that certain departments of a firm must be hived off or sold. Indeed, the paradoxical result of a further definition of plans for co-operation may be exactly opposite to the original plan.

Such extreme results are of course exceptional, but in any case the result of a further definition often shows up integration, specialization, differentiation and parallelization as possibilities or even as definite consequences—not as abstract economic ideas but as sharply defined requirements.

The ways in which companies may co-operate are legion. For instance, agreement between two firms not to employ anyone who has been employed by the other is a form of co-operation. It would be well to bear this in mind when using the word. The subject is enlarged upon in Chapter 3.

MERGERS AND TAKE-OVERS

In explaining the term 'merger' the main thing is to distinguish between a merger and a take-over. In common speech both these concepts are alluded to as mergers, whereas any combination of firms which includes full co-operation is called a concentration. The American terms 'merger' and 'acquisition' are also freely applied to different kinds of co-operation.

We are not aiming here to give a theoretically correct definition of the difference between an acquisition and a merger, but we do want to illustrate the practical difference between a merger and a take-over. A take-over differs from a merger in almost every respect —the consequences of the process of the take-over or merger, the time needed to realize these transactions, the determination of the share exchange or the cash price, the structure at the top, the company development plan and the realization of the aims of the amalgamation.

In fact, they are two totally different transactions, comparable neither in structure nor in appearance. The difference may be defined as follows:

1 TAKE-OVER: As soon as a firm decides, as part of a definite development plan, on full co-operation (amalgamation) with another firm which must adapt itself completely to this plan, we speak of a take-over (acquisition). This therefore implies that the company being taken over unilaterally relinquishes its independence.

2 MERGER: If all those in the amalgamation relinquish independence (absolute independence may be replaced by some measure of independence), and the purposes of the co-operation and the way in which the co-operation will be realized are a matter of common consultation, we speak of a merger. Usually this situation arises where the partners are of approximately the same size, both in the number of employees and in turnover.

Naturally, there are take-overs which are not the result of a company development plan. These are justified only if the take-over is a matter of investment or a 'good buy'. In all other cases it is mainly a question of decorating the Christmas tree.

At the same time we may say that a great number of amalgamations which appear to be take-overs are actually mergers. One need not be much of a psychologist to see that use of the word 'merger' considerably reduces the price of the firm which is to be taken over.

This book is concerned mainly with mergers. The take-over is hardly touched on, in contrast to other (mainly American) literature, where the take-over (acquisition) predominates. This is why in various publications—and now in this book—we have dealt more extensively with mergers, as the most complicated form of co-operation. Up to a point this may have been at the expense of those who are mainly interested in take-overs.

For this reason we should perhaps include a few remarks on take-overs which may prevent misunderstanding in connection with the contents of this book.

1 If take-overs are to be successful, they should almost always form part of a well considered company development plan. This means, for example, that large parts of the working plan for mergers included in Chapter 4 can be ignored, particularly the part dealing with the drawing up of a company development plan for such a plan should already exist.

2 A take-over is a unilateral process. The company which is taking over determines to a considerable extent, the process on the basis of the maximum price which it decides, and on an estimate of what the other party sets as the minimum price. If the owner wishes at all cost to save himself from liquidation, the price of the firm to be taken over may even drop below the break-up value.

   The valuation of the firm being bought should, however—as for mergers—be done on the basis of the results which can be expected from the take-over.

3 The structure of top management presents far fewer problems, will demand less attention and present fewer risks in a take-over than in a merger. The other party is aware it has been taken over and will adapt itself far more easily to a new policy and will not normally create problems.

4 Contractual regulations are much simpler and are limited to a description of the company which is to be taken over, the price and a number of guarantee clauses.

5 The time needed to realize a take-over varies from three weeks to three months; it takes at least a year for a merger to be fully completed.

In this book the take-over will not be dealt with any further. As a process it is comparatively uncomplicated, in sharp contrast to a merger. Nevertheless, much of what is said on mergers can be of great value to those contemplating take-overs. This is why we have dealt so extensively with mergers. The saying 'Never merge unless it is necessary, but if necessary, do it well' is a motto we fully endorse. It should however be noted that in business each step is 'necessary' which promises advantages that cannot be obtained in any other way.

THE LIMITS OF THE BOOK

Finally, we would stress that this book by no means claims to be complete. It aims only at giving a series of systematically arranged ideas. In the course of its construction we have realized more and more how many fields, aspects and problems still remain to be explored.

To enable the reader who is in search of specific experience or expert knowledge to find out whether what he is seeking is included here, without obliging him to read the whole book, the following short survey shows the subjects dealt with and those which have been omitted.

Development Co-operation Merger	Not dealt with (X)	Significance and/or place of subject indicated	Dealt with
Fiscal, legal, conveyancing, actuarial, valuation and accountancy considerations	X	Mergers and succession (55–125) (25–37)	—
Development of society and firm	—	Development (1–7) (8–37)	—
Development investigation	—	Development, co-operation and merger (3–7)	Questionnaires (35–37) (125–128)
Succession	—	Succession (25–37)	(25–37)
Purposes, direction and forms of co-operation	—	Introduction (1–7)	(38–43)
Partial co-operation (in respect of capital; co-operative; by agreement; functional)	X	Co-operation (38–54)	—

Development Co-operation Merger	Not dealt with (X)	Significance and/or place of subject indicated	Dealt with
Partial co-operation: co-operation on complementary product ranges	—	Co-operation (33–54)	(44–54)
Full co-operation: take-over (acquisition)	X	Introduction (1–7)	—
Full co-operation: take-over (take-over bid)	X	—	—
Full co-operation: merger	—	Introduction, development and co-operation (1–54)	(55–161)
do.: choice of merger partners	—	Introduction (1–7)	(55–66)
do.: merger working plan	—	Merger (55–161)	(67–125)
do.: questions to merger partners	—	Merger (55–161)	(125–128)
do.: development plan in case of merger	—	Merger (55–161)	—
do.: valuation in case of merger	—	Merger (55–161)	(137–141)
do.: structure of top management in case of merger	—	Merger (55–161)	(141–150)
do.: commercial policy in case of merger	—	Merger (55–161)	Only for scale-enlarging mergers (150–161)
do.: human problems	—	Merger (55–161)	(142–144)

Finally, we should like to add that we are convinced the direction we have chosen is the right one. The field is extremely interesting; it offers opportunities for satisfying work and the areas which have not yet been developed offer plenty of scope.

2 Development

OPPORTUNITIES FOR DEVELOPMENT

The concept of 'development' occurs frequently in this book. In general, the term means to unfold fully the latent forces inherent in an organism, and implies alterations in the size and structure of the organism. These latent powers are developed by outside nourishment, and are carried out under the influence of factors which may be either favourable or unfavourable. In applying this concept to an industrial firm, development may be said to be, among many other characteristics, the changes in size, the structural relationship between subordinate parts, business relations, and product quality. The development is nourished by finance, labour, etc.

Among the factors which influence development is a composite group for which we usually use the term 'society'. But this, too, is an organism in a state of development. The supplies of such things as accessible raw materials, manpower, intelligence, technical know-how, and social regulations are constantly changing, under the influence of individuals, corporate bodies, enterprises and government.

In using the term development, one should think mainly of interdependence; society influences the company and, in turn the company influences society. This mutual influence on the development of society and business is of great importance when considering the problems dealt with in this book, and especially in this chapter, for experience has shown that successful businessmen and companies keep a close eye on the changes taking place in society. They can also see their own possibilities and limits within the situation in which they find themselves at any given time. On the other hand, the continued existence of the firm may be uncertain if the businessman either does not clearly understand the developments taking place in society, or cannot sufficiently estimate his own position and possibilities. One may therefore distinguish between the active and the passive development of firms, depending on whether growth is directed or whether it is left to take its own course.

If there were ever a chance, for passive development, it is clear that such opportunities are now steadily diminishing. Society is developing at such a rate that no businessman can possibly afford to wait until the effects of any trends have become fully apparent before deciding on their consequences for his own firm. If management fails to keep its ideas in line with social developments, and fails to build up a vision of the influence of these developments on its company, it will lead a hazardous existence or may even succumb to liquidation, take-over or attack. At best, the firm may find itself the victim of a not-too-unfavourable merger.

The following articles are all the result of experiences and impressions gained by firms which were struggling with the problem of development. They should be regarded as possible means of approach. In the article. 'What is the future of smaller and medium-sized firms?' an attempt has been made to give a close analysis of the dynamic development of society. The next article. 'Self-criticism and Independence' aims at indicating a possible way of approach for those businessmen who wish to involve themselves more closely with their company and its alignment with social developments.

Needless to say, a systematic analysis, as described in this article, could never be a substitute for the creativity which is essential in business and which should be the motivating force for the entrepreneur. The data furnished by the analysis, and the ideas it throws up, will enable him to determine the direction his firm should take.

From this it should also be clear that a merger need hardly ever be the only, or the inevitable, solution to the problems of a firm.

WHAT IS THE FUTURE OF SMALLER AND MEDIUM-SIZED FIRMS?

URGENCY OF THE QUESTION

The problem of the future of smaller and medium-sized firms appears to become more urgent each year, and in view of the industrial developments in recent years this is hardly surprising.

There seems no end to wage increases. Every year they exceed the permissible percentage. Productivity lags breathlessly behind, partly because of the uneven increases in productivity throughout industry. These arise when firms with too low a productivity cannot keep up the struggle and disappear, enabling the labour released to be absorbed into companies with greater productivity. The margins—which, owing to lack of 'visibility', were unknown quantities, sometimes for years—are shrinking perceptibly, and the sections of industry which have not yet felt this threat are few and far between.

The EEC, hailed by many as a disaster, has now become a working reality. After a slow start, it is now taken seriously by everyone concerned, and the shades of (sometimes immensely) big companies from distant countries are daily looming closer.

Nevertheless, on studying the actual development of business, it seems that there is no reason for universal pessimism. Many smaller firms are flourishing, although a company may unexpectedly turn out to be doing badly. It may then liquidate or 'merge', in the sense of being taken over. Firms—certainly those with large reserves—are tough, but this does not seem to be a sufficient explanation for the discrepancy between the pessimistic forecasts we have been hearing about for years and the reality of day-to-day business life.

The present situation is obviously symptomatic of some sort of development. What exactly is this development, and what long term trends can we expect during the next few years?

LONG TERM DEVELOPMENTS

The study of trends during recent decades—and some of them originated around or even before 1900—leads one to the following conclusions.

1 The growth of production runs, mechanization, and automation, and the fact that economic obsolescence is getting further and further ahead of technical obsolescence, have led to increasing capital investment. Capital investment as a percentage of National Income is rising and compared to the individual consumer, industry and governments are becoming increasingly important customers.

2 The purchasing power of the general public is increasing—a trend which is accompanied by social emancipation. The proportion of income which can be freely spent is also growing.

3 The gap between the producer and the consumer is widening, yet, at the same time, it is being bridged by advertising. It has become imperative to advertise in order to obtain high, but technically minimum, sales. It is also becoming the only means of competition in mass production—the percentage cost of selling set against the total cost is steadily increasing.

4 The perfecting of transport and communication techniques is enlarging the scale of operations. The development of air transport, bulk transport, teleprinting, the mobility of trade and international information on supply and demand trends, and market developments are all breaking up regional restrictions.

Views differ on the date by which the EEC will have become a total reality. Many even feel—the wish may be father to the thought—that in the present political situation it will never be possible. The question of whether Britain will or will not join the EEC also remains unresolved, and its possible consequences have not been analysed.

It is possible to study the year 1968 in detail and to try and evaluate the consequences of wage increases for a particular firm. The conclusion may be that things will not turn out too badly or that one must wait and see. Of course, it is true that, within the near future, little can be said with absolute certainty on any of these subjects. If, however, present trends continue during the next decade, the optimum size of companies may be expected to increase dramatically. Growing internationalization under pressure of these forces will be inevitable. At the same time, profit margins will continue to fall.

PRIORITIES FOR THE SMALLER FIRM:
THREATENED CATEGORIES

Present trends raise the question of whether there is still any room for the smaller firm. This question cannot be answered in general terms. That part of business which is composed of the smaller and medium-sized firms covers an extremely varied conglomeration of companies of all sizes, which cannot be realistically compared with one another. In attempting to answer the question, some system of grouping, according to certain characteristics, is necessary. In this way one can find starting points from which to draw conclusions for a particular firm.

It is certain that there is a large group of smaller and medium-sized firms in the UK which has reason to be seriously concerned about the future. Among them are all those companies where management organization, production techniques and marketing or financial structure are inadequate. These firms have low profit margins and owe their continued existence either to protective measures or to temporary or gradually declining factors. Some of these factors are historical ties with buyers, labour scarcity, exceptional but one-sided qualities of managers, qualities of former managers, etc. When it comes to 'the survival of the fittest' these firms will be amongst the first to go. In practice, not much can be done about such companies; they have generally reached their present state for a very good reason.

A second category is that of firms where the succession is not sufficiently assured. In the UK, one may say that many of the smaller and medium-sized companies are still family firms. Society and business may be expected to become more and more dynamic and complicated. This means that the demands on leadership will continue to increase, that the pressure on a balanced management will continue to grow, and that any disturbance in this balance will weigh many times more heavily than in the past.

How many smaller firms have really settled the matter of succession, not only of the manager or managers but also of the top executives? How many of the smaller companies are there, where the division of shares after hereditary transmission is such that it forms a potential source of difficulty, even when it does not directly affect the executive management of the company? How many of these businesses have effectively adapted their financial structure to the latent tax obligations which appear with a merger, sale, liquidation or hereditary transmission? Companies which conduct their business under such circumstances are like tight-rope-walkers who refuse to use a safety-net.

A third category of firms which should seriously consider the matter of future development is those which either manufacture products that could be produced at lower cost by larger firms, or products on which other companies can calculate a larger percentage of research or development costs in their actual price, or a bigger percentage of sales costs. These are the companies which are still a long way from the optimum size for the range of articles they produce and can be found in almost all branches of industry. They are threatened especially by the tremendous leeway they already have to make up in their growth towards optimum size. Also, owing to the speed with which developments take place, such a firm frequently cannot realize the extent of the growth necessary for its continued independence.

The fact that bigger firms calculate higher percentages of development costs and sales costs may, for a long time, give the impression that a firm can still compete and can keep up with its prices. Nevertheless, in almost all these cases a company is eating into its own future.

Comparing these three categories, we see that the danger threatening the firms differ from one category to another. Of the first group (marginal firms) the greater number will not be able to avert the dangers threatening them during the next few years. One might even say that during the past years employers and employees have demonstrated their agreement on this point. Of the second category (insufficiently assured succession) the continued existence is tied up with a number of uncertain factors which will only become clear in the future. Rationally speaking, it is generally possible to solve problems of succession, proportional ownership of shares and tax problems. Emotionally, however, they often cannot be solved. The business belonging to an owner/manager has become a part of himself; interventions in the firm are felt to be practically surgical operations on his own body (see also pages 25–30).

During the past few years there have been many instances of companies which have not been able to settle these problems during the life of their owner/manager and which have disappeared or been taken over. During the next few years there will, doubtless, be many more such cases.

The dangers threatening the third group (too small) are of a different nature again. The threat is just as inevitable as it is to the first category. It will, however, be much more gradual, and will show itself at different moments in different industries and branches of industry. For instance, those firms which owe their strength more to their regional position than to protective measures will generally experience this threat at a later stage. In the Common Market area there are population centres, each with its own pattern of behaviour and consumption. Within these centres, regional positions based on knowledge of the market, special characteristics of the available labour, etc., will be maintained for a long time. It is, however, incorrect to think that the advantages of a regional position will be maintained indefinitely. In due course they will inevitably disappear.

CONSEQUENCES FOR THE SMALLER FIRM: SAFE CATEGORIES

In addition to the group of smaller and medium-sized firms which is facing a difficult period, there is a further group whose existence does not depend on internationalization and on the development of an optimum size.

In other words, there will still be room for smaller firms and a need for certain products which can only be developed and manufactured in a smaller unit. In this context we shall not consider the marginal firms which are at present in any particular group. No matter what the developments may be, there will always be new marginal firms, or existing companies which become marginal. We are here concerned with those firms which, in the products or services they supply and in the character of their organization, differ fundamentally from the larger firms. These are the firms which—even if they grow—will never become competitors of the big companies (or vice versa), as they cover other needs. They are the super-specialists among companies.

These are, in the first place, companies with strong regional outlets, and sometimes, inevitable local manufacture, where there is a clear ceiling on sales. In this context, one may think of retail trade in luxury articles in the bigger towns, of small local building firms, local transport firms, workshops and other local businesses. These are the companies specializing in a restricted market—restricted either by the nature of the product or the nature of the market.

A second group is formed by those companies which have an upper limit to sales, not because of any regional character but due to necessity based on the ability of the particular industry to change models frequently. Many small firms dealing in fashionable goods will always more or less hold their own amidst their bigger companions. The cost of luxurious products also sets an upper limit to sales, which makes the business unviable to those manufacturers who have to depend on bulk sales. Such products as ready-made clothes, furniture, leatherware, and certain sectors of the textile and metal industry often come within this range, which can only operate in a limited size.

The third category involves mass production, of items of which the usage, even within a big unit, is not large enough to justify production within that unit. This is a typical form of super-specialism. The manufacture of shock-absorbers is one example, but this type of limited-size company is also found elsewhere, particularly in the metal industry (e.g. the manufacture of car bodies in the US).

A fourth group might be described as the 'custom-built' firms. They simply aim at meeting the individual purchaser's requirements. The buyer indicates his needs and often the method of manufacture. He dictates what should be supplied and in what way. Many of the smaller construction firms—especially those grouped around the large towns—will continue to make a good living from this sort of business. This type of operation is also possible in the transport sector. To a lesser extent, there should be some room for 'made-to-measure' work in almost all branches of industry.

CONCLUSION

It must be stressed that there is certainly a future in industrial life for the smaller and medium-sized company. Society would be the poorer if the possibilities of variety offered by the smaller firm were to disappear. However, there will also continue to be room in a mass-production society, which would guarantee a living to firms of a relatively small size. For some categories, the small size might even be a prerequisite for continued existence. Strangely enough, the desire to expand may also form a threat to a company.

Against this, there is the fact that some of the smaller and medium-sized companies would do well to re-orientate themselves. This might mean considering the possibility of expansion. It could mean —and this is too often forgotten—considering possibilities of some kind of specialization. In practice, however, both the growth required to attain an optimum size and the shifting in policy which is to lead to a different kind of industry often prove almost impossible.

It is therefore certain that, no matter what may be said or

written, many smaller and medium-sized firms will in due course disappear. If this is so, it must be in the interest of every businessman to analyse his own firm's position accurately at the earliest possible stage. Even if there is no potential in the present situation, there are still many possibilities of ensuring a favourable outcome by suitable development. But these are essentially 'long term'; they will not miraculously take place from one day to the next. What is important is that one should 'see' the way one's area of industry is heading. There is usually still time and room enough to adapt one's firm to what will eventually be required by society and also to 'choose one's position' and 'form up'—doing this may be considered essential to successful entrepreneurship.

SELF-CRITICISM AND INDEPENDENCE

IS THERE STILL A NEED FOR INDEPENDENCE?

Superficially it appears that nowadays businesses feel less need for independence than they used to do. The number of mergers rises every year. It seems, therefore, that the businessman is taking the loss of his independence more and more lightly.

On the other hand, small operators, and also many of the not-so-small independent businessmen, continue to draw an income from their firm which is less than they would be able to draw as wage-earners elsewhere. This can only be explained by assuming that managing one's own business yields a psychological—rather than a material—income.

For the owner of a larger firm this generally does not apply. For him the risk concerns capital rather than income. The need for independence has been sublimated into maintaining the business for his family and descendants. The aim for independence shows itself in an absolute refusal to sell any part of the self-established firm.

It is wrong to conclude that there is less desire for independence today. The great majority of businessmen are very strongly attached to their companies and are so set on continued independence that a 'need for independence' is a somewhat inadequate description of their feelings. The self-created company is part of the family. It bears a personal stamp and its characteristics frequently reflect the character of its manager/founder. Separating the entrepreneur and the firm is sometimes comparable to the surgical operation required to make Siamese twins into two separate people.

THE NEED FOR LARGER BUSINESS UNITS

At the present time, the intimate connection between the entrepreneur/owner and the company is assailed on every side by pronouncements which come down to one thing—there must be larger business units. From the many speeches and addresses on this subject, the statement of the board of the Dutch National Investment Bank in its annual report of 1963 on small companies is typical. It concluded that 'a small firm by definition is one where the businessman is competent .. himself to provide good, all-round leadership for his company, can concern himself with all kinds of details, and is able for the greater part to keep his eye on the business directly.' With regard to these firms it went on: 'One may, however, wonder whether there will still be room for such firms in the future, now that the influence of large business units is increasing and new or bigger demands can, to a greater extent, and more easily than hitherto, be met by increased production of large well established companies.'

As authors such as Galbraith and Zahn have often described, a situation will arise in which the first priority of the business will not be increased production, but the problems of selling and distributing large output in order to maintain full employment.

For many small firms it is a quite impossible task to solve these distribution problems in the competitive struggle which in the EEC is getting ever fiercer, owing to the ending of import duties and the perfecting of means of communication. No other argument is therefore necessary to see that larger business units are certainly favoured to some extent.

PRESSURE ON BUSINESSMEN

The average businessman, faced with these arguments and considerations, will not deny the logic of forming larger units of business. But, against this logical reasoning there is the emotional—unreasoned—reaction of not wishing to accept this conclusion for the self-made business. In the field of tension between emotion and reason, reason does not stand much of a chance. Entrepreneurship is never a matter of rational calculation, but rather of the following of intuitive ideas which are tested and shaped by rational thought and calculations. A conclusion that the firm should be merged into a larger unit is rejected, along with the entire reasoning about increasing the size of business units.

All other kinds of re-orientation are likewise omitted, and the businessman seeks to defend his independence in maintaining the *status quo*. He thus chooses the conservative path which generally promotes exactly what he wished to avoid.

THE DANGERS OF CONSERVATISM

To be conservative historically implies reliability. When it is a matter of the valuation of assets on balance-sheets, this may possibly be true. Conservatism in business policy, however, has never been a great advantage, and should nowadays be regarded as highly perilous.

One cannot continue to base one's policies on circumstances pertaining five years ago—on the cost of labour and capital dating from that period; on consumption habits and methods of distribution of that—not too far distant—time. It should be remembered that it is not the factors within the firm which feed the tendency to larger business units, but the world surrounding the firm which is changing. This demands a change in the firm's attitude towards the surrounding world, i.e. 'an adapted policy'.

Conservatism in these circumstances leads to a downwards spiral from which after a while, it may be impossible to escape unaided. By insufficiently adapting policy to altered circumstances, the gross profit margins fall below the level necessary to meet expenses for renewals and replacements. If technical factors require some investment or external financing which is impossible or too expensive, the only way out is to merge, or even be taken over by another firm.

SELF-CRITICISM: PREREQUISITE FOR INDEPENDENCE

The alternative to conservatism is a flexible policy, i.e. a policy adapted to the development of the surrounding society. Developing such a policy is anything but easy. It is much simpler to maintain existing policy than it is continually to be seeking a creative answer to the development of society. Conservatism therefore might also be called choosing the path of least resistance.

The choice of a flexible policy requires self-criticism: the ability to consider continually and critically what has been attained and thus to look for possibilities for the future. From these possibilities a selection must be made which is best suited to the firm and its management.

The practical application of critical self-analysis begins with 'study of turnover', that is, the source of the means by which the firm exists, strengthens and grows. Studying turnover does not simply mean having a look at the output reached by the firm and then guessing a future trend. It means a critical consideration of the results obtained per article over the course of years with various separate customers, the influence of substitute articles and of national and foreign competing products. This will make well-founded forecasts possible.

From the size and make-up of turnover in the recent past and near future (a total period of between eight and ten years is usually sufficient) the examination is directed at the way in which the level of sales has been reached. This means assessing whether the commercial conditions are sound, by examining the size of orders, product range, modernity of design, quality of customers, gross margin of profit, etc.

In the third phase of the investigation, attention is paid to the technical processes by which output is secured. Has the organization of production always been attuned to the sales requirements, and what technical organizations will be required for the turnover expected in the future?

Not infrequently, one finds that the production apparatus and its organization really belong to a quite different policy from the one on which the commercial organization and the turnover expectations are based. In this way, demands made on the cash flow brought in by sales will be unnecessarily high, and will, therefore, not leave enough for the capital investment which must be paid from these funds.

'Examination of investment plans' is the fourth stage in our critical self-analysis. Here we must see which investments will be necessary for the various alternatives open in the choice of policy. Critical self-analysis aims at putting these alternatives to the test, and selecting the one which, in view of the expected development of society, offers the best chances for the continued independence of the firm. Considering the investments which would be a necessary part of the alternatives open is the last step in assembling the material needed to see whether desirabilities and possibilities can be reconciled.

The proof of this can be found in 'financial analysis'. In this fifth phase of the investigation, turnover, expenses, repayment of loans and investment plans are all expressed in monetary units and then compared. In this way one can assess whether the turnover furnishes the means required to realize the investment programme.

Where a choice is possible between alternative policies, it should at that stage be determined which policies offer the required turnover. Provided, therefore, that self-criticism is undertaken in time, it becomes a pre-condition of independence. Where the need for independence is put first, a critical self-analysis can show which policy will lead to a preservation of this independence.

WHERE IS INDEPENDENCE POSSIBLE?

In general, it is hard to say which firms reach the conclusion that an independent existence is possible in the changing social circumstances which result from the full-employment policy, the Common Market, automation and telecommunication. We can, however, on the grounds of experience, make a cautious attempt at such a distinction for smaller firms. Here we find several types of policy under which companies can be small and remain so in these changing circumstances.

Four groups stand out:

1 Companies which are strongly regional as regards either sales or labour. The element in policy which makes independence possible here is that this connection with a town or district is consciously pursued, for, in general, the local market disappears under the circumstances mentioned above (see pages 16–17). But, if from the possibilities at hand one can choose a local one, and make oneself strong in this respect, then a policy has been found which will enable a small firm to remain independent.

Such a policy is found in the following groups:

(a) Contractors.
(b) Engineering works.
(c) Local transport.
(d) Printing.
(e) Concrete manufacturers.

2 Companies which frequently change their models due to fashion. The more fashionable the company, the smaller it can, even should, be.

Such firms are to be found, *inter alia*, in sectors specializing in the production of:

(a) Ready-made wear.
(b) Furniture.
(c) Leather goods.
(d) Spectacle frames, etc.

3 This concerns mass-producing articles which are, nevertheless, needed in small quantities which are not economic for large companies to manufacture.

The element of policy here is to aim at ingenious manufacture of a limited range. Once the firm allows itself to extend its range, its small size and independence are no longer compatible.

Examples:

(a) Machine tools.
(b) Insulating materials.

4 Companies manufacturing components according to buyer's specification. The element of policy making independence and lack of size compatible here is the aim to meet all the special requirements of the customer. Once large orders are accepted, a hybrid situation will arise (insufficient flexibility for special orders and too high costs for large orders) which will not long survive the changing demands of society.

Instances of this type of firm are found in:

(a) Engineering.
(b) Transport.
(c) Repair shops, etc.

This list of industrial groups may be greatly extended, for this is not a matter of technology but of specialized policy.

A NEW FORM OF SERVICE BY EMPLOYERS' ORGANIZATIONS

Because of the continuous changes in the development of society, it is not sufficient to draw up a self-analysis only once. It would seem— a work group of the Royal Institute of Engineers (in Holland) has already reported on this—that data must be compiled periodically to show the firm's position with regard to the choice between co-operation and independence. This means that an added sacrifice is required from the management, a sacrifice which should be regarded as the insurance premium necessary for choosing the best course for the firm's policy. There may well be financial and/or organizational obstacles, especially in small companies. On the other hand, it is just these small firms (and the medium-sized family companies) which will profit most from the information which periodical analysis would supply.

One may safely say that it would be a loss to society if small firms, simply because they did not understand the situation in time, were forced to stop work or to merge into a larger body and therefore no longer be able to offer those special services which only they can perform at a profit.

As such an analysis is a task which is certainly not a full-time job, organizations—such as trade associations—might more frequently assist their members in these self-analyses on a collective basis, and with sufficient guarantees for confidential treatment.

CONCLUSION

The manager who, in this rapidly and drastically changing society, wishes to maintain the independence of his company, must be open to self-criticism and banish all elements of conservatism. Only by systematically reviewing—as sketched above—what has been attained, and by analysing what is attainable, is it possible to build up a flexible policy.

Or, to put it briefly: self-criticism is the basis of independence.

CONTINUITY IN MANAGEMENT AND OWNERSHIP

At the beginning of this chapter we stated that the successful firm shows understanding of the developments of society as well as of its own possibilities and limitations.

In the life of a company, as in the life of every other organism, there are periods of growth, stagnation or decline. In other words, there will probably be times when understanding of the situation is lacking.

On studying the firms which are going through a period of stagnation or decline we find that there are many reasons for this, such as a lack of capability in one or more aspects of management. Stagnation may, however, also be caused by the fact that the company's structure has not been adapted to the changes in society. But, repeated experience of companies in such a condition shows that expected changes in management have often also played their part in causing this stagnation. There are two possible reasons for this:

1 In talking about the future, management often closes its eyes to the obvious necessity of providing for a successor.
2 The management has not succeeded in reducing to discussion level the obvious need for a change in group policy, which might perhaps necessitate some kind of co-operation or merger. Thoughts about the future are blocked by numerous, mainly emotional, considerations.

We have found, by experience, that a business development plan can help in such cases. It encourages clear thinking about the future, and as clarity increases, there is less room left for emotion. A systematic investigation of possibilities often shows directions of development which, up till then, had not been realized. A clear definition of the existing risks, and those which may be expected, and their financial consequences, enforces definite thought about the measures or actions which should be taken.

We have drawn on our experience in dealing with this kind of problem in 'A contribution towards dealing with the problem of succession'. Additional aspects to be covered in a development investigation in cases where there are also problems of succession, have been included in the questionnaire shown in the last section of this chapter. These will also indicate certain areas which still remain to be investigated.

A CONTRIBUTION TOWARDS DEALING WITH THE PROBLEM OF SUCCESSION

THE CONCEPT OF SUCCESSION

Contrary to the more restricted meaning usually assigned to the word 'succession', the concept is used here in a much wider sense.

Problems of succession will here be taken to include all those problems which might arise in a firm when there is a change or transfer of management, of capital, or of both. This comparatively wide definition shows that a number of seemingly different situations—among them succession in the more limited sense of the word—have certain problems in common which can be dealt with in this context. A common characteristic of all these is the transfer of management and/or capital.

The problem of succession, thus defined, does not only occur in cases of death and inheritance, but also when management is transferred due to long illness or retirement. It happens, too, in those situations where, in order to maintain progress, transactions must be carried out which result in a transfer of management and/or capital, such as mergers, take-overs, sale, changes in the legal structure, transfer to a new owner, admission of partners, new managers.

THE IMPORTANCE OF SETTLING THE SUCCESSION

Recently, the future of the small and medium-sized firm has been discussed more and more frequently—with good reason. Without going deeply into the developments of society (illustrated by the increase in the optimum size of undertakings, growing internationalization and the general tendency for margins to drop) it is clear that this group of companies is facing a difficult period. In fact, it seems certain that a considerable number of smaller, and also medium-sized, companies will disappear during the next decade, because they will no longer be able to keep up the struggle for survival.

If this disappearance is the result—in no matter what way—of a marginal condition (inadequate management, organization, production technique, marketing, financial structure, etc.), it may, from a social point of view, be called a constructive development as it will lead to increased productivity. Where sound firms with good chances of development disappear due to factors other than economic ones, then this is a loss to society.

There is no doubt that society is subject to big changes. Business is becoming increasingly dynamic and the demands made on the flexibility of the company and the capacity of the management are increasing every year. During coming years, every business will, more than ever, have to plan carefully if it is to survive. In this connection, the problem of succession presents a great potential danger to the smaller and medium-sized firm. Many otherwise sound and remunerative firms disappear or decline for the simple reason that little or nothing has been done about establishing succession.

It is also virtually certain that a large majority of small and medium-sized companies is daily threatened by the same fate. Risks are taken which vary from a wavering 'inter-regnum', unnecessarily heavy financial sacrifices and other hitches in the company's continuity, to winding-up or the final sale of the company. Among the enterprises threatened in this way are not only the one-man firms, but also a large number of so-called 'family companies'.

The possibilities of separating management and capital in the smaller family firms should not be over-estimated. Tax regulations concerning influential shareholders, difficulties in preserving the balance between conflicting groups, dangerous minority positions due to the small number of shareholders, psychological obstacles and regulations and the practice of blocking the transfer of shares all render the small limited company less mobile in practice than it is in theory.

PROBLEMS OF SUCCESSION

In transferring management and capital attention must be paid to many factors. These include legal and contractual requirements, taxation, moral duties, differences in personality, capacity, etc. Any company which is to be transferred will run into economic and commercial danger if these obstacles are not dealt with in time and suitable precautions taken. Some of the chief hazards which may arise are listed below.

A: DANGERS RELATED TO THE CONTRACTUAL STRUCTURE OF THE BUSINESS

If the sole proprietor of a firm dies without having made contractual agreements and/or provisions regarding the capital and continuation of the firm, some of his heirs may well demand to be paid out their shares in the capital of the firm. This could result in a forced sale of the business or its component parts, or its contraction.

The same kind of danger threatens in the case of a partnership, if partners die, or leave for any reason, and there is no agreement whereby their capital is paid out over a reasonable period.

If no provisions have been made concerning the manner in which successors will be nominated on the death or departure of directors of a limited company, the result may be that people who are quite unqualified may suddenly be called upon to nominate a successor. Any mistakes in the choice of management are generally very costly.

A lack of effective regulations, whether in the Articles of Association or elsewhere, to prevent undesirable changes in control resulting from the transfer of shares in the limited company, brings a risk of unexpected events which may suddenly render the position of the company and its management uncertain, with all the disastrous consequences this may have.

B: DANGERS CONCERNING TAXATION

If a sole proprietor, one partner, or the influential shareholder in a company has, for years, directed his energies solely to the development of the firm, and has paid little or no attention to the accumulation of personal capital outside the firm, retirement will immediately bring major Capital Gains Tax, Estate Duty and other associated problems. Very careful drafting by professional advisers of all formal documents concerning the constitution of the firm, its contracts, and the devolution or settlement of proprietors' interests or shares in the business is essential to minimize the impact of taxation on the occurrence of future events.

C: DANGERS OF INADEQUATE LIFE ASSURANCE OR RETIREMENT PROVISIONS

Sole traders, partnerships, and private companies frequently defer making adequate provision for the sake of present expansion. Catching up on these provisions later may mean that far too great a charge on profits must be made in later years. If the businessman dies prematurely, the consequences of inadequate provisions are even worse, sometimes so bad as to make the continuation of a company impossible; at the same time, obtaining credit will become more difficult.

The income earned by the son who is to be the successor may also be kept down to strengthen the company financially. This may mean, however, that the son cannot build up the funds which he may, in due course, require to take over from his father. In consequence, when the parents die, the company will be divided with his co-inheritors and the chance of adequate and effective succession is greatly diminished.

In general, the life and death of the businessman and his wife frequently prove of great importance to the continuity of the small firm.

D: DANGERS OF PERSONAL ORGANIZATION

The leadership provided by the founder or entrepreneur/owner who has built up his firm into a flourishing concern is strictly personal. The impetus provided by this leadership cannot be transferred to a new leader from one day to the next. If the transfer of leadership is not prepared for in time, it is almost certain that the firm will need a long transitional period to recover from the change.

E: DANGERS INHERENT IN THE CHOICE OF SUCCESSOR

Even in cases when a successor must be chosen at an inopportune time, it is still important to consider which persons are best qualified to succeed. Only in this way can unqualified or unprepared members of the next generation be prevented from obtaining—by right of succession or because of fluctuations in family relationships—a great deal of power, and perhaps causing irreparable losses during the time they will need to learn their work. A struggle for power also forms a considerable threat to the firm and should be prevented by timely measures.

F: DANGERS OF A PSYCHOLOGICAL NATURE

The owner/manager, partner or influential shareholder, and—although generally to a lesser extent—even professional management, usually find it a difficult task to transfer their leadership effectively.

Many executives perform their work with great success, but it would be impossible to find two who do it in exactly the same way. Each one however, is convinced that his way is the best, if not the only one possible. This characteristic is, possibly, essential for success, but it is one which also considerably complicates the transfer of leadership. In a family business, this may sorely tax the strength of the company; sometimes, the period prior to taking-over may prove too much for the successor, so that the problems which will arise when the actual transfer must take place are further aggravated.

CAUSES FOR INADEQUATE PROVISION FOR SUCCESSION

In a large number of smaller and medium-sized firms the matter of succession has been settled inadequately or not at all. Risks, like those discussed in the preceding pages, generally come as a complete surprise at the—equally unexpected—moment that succession must be decided.

Why are such situations allowed to arise? The first important reason is the psychological resistance of all human beings to facing the fact that one day they will be dead. This provides a block to tackling problems which will arise on or around the moment of their decease. Of course, arrangements which must be made for a possible succession are just as vital as others which occur in a business.

The second reason is that so many complicated problems arise which do not belong to the daily work of the businessman, yet require sound knowledge and are closely inter-connected. We live in a society of increasing specialization and the problem of co-ordinating specialization—particularly in smaller firms—is almost insoluble. Seldom can the accountant or the tax expert, the lawyer, or the insurance expert, or any other specialist, individually offer the integrated advice which the businessman requires when he is settling problems connected with his succession. He himself is required to sum up everything, and co-ordinate the specialists. However, very few people have the perseverance to make full and satisfactory arrangements.

Another reason—or excuse—for making inadequate provisions is that the incumbent is dealing with a more or less distant, and therefore uncertain future. This future is usually only seen in terms of general expectations and never, or hardly ever, in definite terms.

DEVELOPMENT PLAN: FINDING A SOLUTION

If the reasons given above for making inadequate provisions for succession are correct, it does not look as if the situation can be easily altered. It seems most unlikely that the tendency to specialize in different problems will lessen in the near future. And the psychological obstacles to thinking about succession will certainly not disappear overnight.

Any contribution towards more effective arrangements for succession must offer realism as opposed to emotionalism as far as specific projections of future possibilities are concerned. It must also bring the means of co-ordinating specialities.

Such a contribution is provided by a quantitative picture of the most probable economic/financial development of the company during the next five or ten years. This development plan may provide the central concept which enables the businessman and his experts to select from the large number of starting-points, a few which are mutually compatible. It also helps to set down the concrete problems for which each of the experts must try to provide solutions in his own field.

DRAWING UP A DEVELOPMENT PLAN

In drawing up a development plan we may single out the following stages:

Investigation

This is an analysis of the present situation. It falls into two parts.

First, the actual position of the company in its general context, and the potential for development—theoretically and in broad outline. For this we shall have to dig into the past, where we must look into the development of turnover, of profit margins, of utilization of capital, of distribution channels and sales methods, of production techniques, and of product development. These, expressed in financial terms, should present a clear picture of the way in which the company has developed to its present state.

Second, the investigation stage includes the examination of such data as the relation between private capital and the capital in the firm, the incidence of taxation and its minimization, the insurance provisions made in various fields, structure of the family, any provisions regarding estate duty, company law, law of succession and even marriage law in those countries where relevant. If such an analysis is carried out with care, the main risks to the continuity of the firm at the moment of succession will be clearer. This is still, however, not sufficient; future risks must be localized and provided for.

Forecast
From the present position of the company and after considering expected developments of society generally, we must now draw up a forecast for the turnover from which we shall later be able to project future balance sheets, and profit and loss accounts. Naturally, such a prognosis is not an easy matter. As a rule it is only possible and meaningful after the matter has been fully discussed within the business. We may find that there are such wide differences of opinion that we must draw up alternative prognoses which must each be further developed. It is certainly no reflection on a business when such divergencies of view exist.

The economic viability of these (possibly alternative) prognoses is then examined by studying how the margins of profit, current production, selling costs, and investment must develop, if the examined policy is to be successful and the expected turnover attained. Investment in fixed assets and working capital will be required.

These prognoses are not complete until the management of the company has agreed on the alternatives to be developed. It is quite possible that, at this stage, one or more alternatives will drop out because of unacceptable consequences. From the forecasts one can, with the help of comparative figures—which may vary from one company to another, and which can be obtained from Balance Sheets and Profit and Loss Accounts of former years—project the Balance Sheets and Profit and Loss Accounts for the next five to eight years. This provides a picture of the future profitability and liquidity and also shows at what times capital will be required and when funds can be withdrawn from the company. The need for financing can thus be determined and one can see whether the plans contained in the prognoses can be carried through independently or whether outside capital will be required. If this is so then it must be decided whether this will create a capital structure which is viable in the light of the expected development of society. Generally, at this stage only one of the various policies remains which can be agreed on by all concerned.

Having reached this stage, it is much easier to study the consequences of various events or expected developments. We can, for instance, now see what, at any given moment, will be the consequences of a crisis—what will be the approximate situation when the present owner/manager retires, when the present legal structure of the company will begin to show limitations. Such a perspective will also show whether planned developments are possible or whether a decrease in development possibilities should be taken into account. It is also then possible to analyse whether a merger or some other form of co-operation should be considered to compensate for this decrease or limitation in development. If so, one can—although only in very broad outline—already consider the financial, legal and taxational consequences of the course decided.

USE OF DEVELOPMENT PLAN WHEN SETTLING SUCCESSION

It has been found that, in drawing up the development plan, the attention of the businessman is often drawn away from himself and his own mortality to the firm and its continuity. Many psychological problems are thus circumnavigated. The future has been defined and the specialists can be provided with a lucid document giving them the chance to advise, from their own expertise, on the basis of a uniform and definite view of the future, drawn up with and by the company. The use of a development plan may lead to the most widely ranging decisions, both concerning actual management and all the arrangements which can be made with a view to succession. An enumeration of all these possibilities and combinations of possibilities would carry things too far—even supposing it were possible—so this chapter is restricted to the brief description of a single case concerning a smaller business. The problems of succession and development are often extremely difficult in a smaller firm.

In a wholesale company, which had been a partnership with two partners, and which was to be converted into a limited company, a request was made to consider the problem of succession. It appeared that each partner had bequeathed his entire estate to his wife, although two sons had already entered the firm and it was the

intention that they should succeed the father/partners. If a will is
made, such an arrangement is quite common and in itself has nothing to do with a development plan. It will, however, at once be
clear that a will of this kind could not do the firm any good. In
drawing up the development plan it was found that, not only was
the present situation of the company such that the possibilities of
growth during the next five to ten years were tremendous, but also
that the profitability would probably increase by between three
and five hundred per cent. The amounts required for investment
were not especially high, although at certain moments which could
be determined to within approximately six months, larger amounts
might be required to finance the take-over of smaller firms. Moreover, it was found that, apart from the present activities, various
new interests might be developed, as the company would attain a
size which would justify the undertaking of such new developments.
The result of all this was that the conversion of the firm had to be
done in such a way that not one, but two limited companies were
created. A number of purposes could then be realized:

1 The business risk was spread in such a way that the activities
   carrying the greater contingent risks were isolated in a subsidiary company, thereby protecting in some measure the
   capital of the parent company. Such day-to-day activities
   could be conducted in the subsidiary company and financed
   from the capital, or conducted with the plant, of the parent
   company.

2 New activities could be undertaken in newly-established
   subsidiary companies which meant that the possibilities for
   growth of the new concern were bigger. It also meant that the
   risks incurred by the new companies would be restricted to
   these companies and the capital tied up in them.

3 Given the expected increase in profits, it would become
   possible to take such measures that insurance premiums for
   death and transfer of capital were reduced to normal proportions, while both partners could also accumulate such
   private capital that, in the event of any unforeseen circumstances, the continuity of the business would no longer be
   threatened by taxation.

All these measures were, at first sight, anything but obvious.
The final picture of the company and the measures taken were

very different from those which had at first been envisaged. The original plans for the future proved to be vulnerable, particularly when the favourable profit growth was realized and the investigation highlighted, as planned, was able to highlight what risks could result from set-backs that had not been anticipated. The development plan enabled such steps to be taken as not only to ensure profitable expansion for the companies but also to enable them to make provision for such occurrences.

This is an example of what can be achieved, provided there is close co-operation between the various specialists. Such co-operation is a prerequisite for any really satisfactory arrangements. Any arrangement which takes into account all aspects cannot, by definition, be developed starting from just one single speciality. In this sense, the use of a development plan can considerably lighten the problems arising in settling matters of succession.

A TYPICAL QUESTIONNAIRE

Both for development investigation, and for the study of succession problems, questionnaires are frequently used; these are either submitted to the management of the company or more often used by the investigator as a 'check list'. They are, of course, drawn up for individual cases. Nevertheless, certain parts of these questionnaires keep recurring. To give an impression of the data generally required for any development investigation an example of such a questionnaire is included here, followed by a list of subjects which must also be discussed if there are problems of succession to be dealt with.

DEVELOPMENT INVESTIGATION

1 Detailed and audited accounts for the last five years.
2 Management accounts for the last five years.
3 Budgeted accounts for the last five years and for the current year.
4 Cash flow and statistical analyses for the last five years and for the current year.

5 Recent valuation reports on plant, land and buildings, leases, stock, etc.

6 Turnover and profit margins over the last five years, divided into product groups, customer groups, size of orders, etc. *Note:* This division should be done in such a way that diverging developments can be followed separately.

7 Prognoses of turnover and profit margins over the next five years, divided again into product groups, customer groups, size of orders, etc.

Comments of management.
(*a*) If present policy is continued.
(*b*) In case of any alterations in policy (e.g. new products, more standardization, increase in exports, etc.).

Comments of management.

8 Departmental analysis covering the last five years, number of staff, etc.

9 Prognosis of current production costs.

(*a*) If present policy is continued.
(*b*) In case of any alterations in policy.

Comments of management.

10 Capital investment required during the next five years—for replacement assets, working capital and research and development expenditure, in order of priority.

(*a*) Under present policy.
(*b*) In case of alterations in policy.

Comments of management.

11 Financial forecasts for next five years, with particular reference to stock levels, debtors, liquid resources, creditors, etc.

(*a*) What is the profit expectation; how will this profit be used?
(*b*) What will become available through depreciation?
(*c*) What plans, undertakings and agreements have been made regarding old-age pensions and distribution of profits to personnel, recipients of bonuses, directors and shareholders?

PROBLEMS OF SUCCESSION

1 Memorandum and Articles of Association of Companies. Management agreements and documents relating to succession, the background to them.
2 Shareholdings. Voting agreements and other agreements between shareholders, etc.
3 Trusts, family arrangements and testamentary dispositions regarding shares, personal capital, where relevant.
4 Personal capital of owner/directors, or partners.
5 Family of owner/directors or partners.
6 Intentions and possibilities regarding succession.

3 Co-operation

AIMS, DIRECTIONS AND FORMS OF CO-OPERATION

A development investigation in many companies leads to the conclusion that some kind of co-operation with another company is required for the continuity of the firm. Such a conclusion creates more problems than it solves. We must therefore look for rational considerations which will offer reassurance and certainty on the road to co-operation and will also act as a check against precipitate action.

This rational support may be found, first of all, in the development investigation itself, for this shows fairly accurately which problems need co-operation, and also what this co-operation is required to yield. In other words: the development investigation will give a schedule of requirements for co-operation.

The directors of the firm are now faced with the task of having to draw up and effect a form of co-operation suited to their business, which will meet these requirements. For this, a list of the possible partners and types of co-operation appropriate is necessary, so that a wrong choice of form or partner is not made through lack of knowledge of more attractive alternatives. The strength and the weakness of each of these forms must also be realized, in order that the conclusions of the development investigation may be translated into a policy of co-operation which is directed towards a clear purpose and backed by the conviction of its need by the parties involved.

'Bird's-eye view of co-operation' (below) provides a short survey of aims, directions and forms of co-operation. In each case there is a brief indication of the different problems which can arise when two firms decide to open negotiations. Every case is different and each will require its own particular solution.

BIRD'S-EYE VIEW OF CO-OPERATION

ALONE OR TOGETHER?

The changes in economic conditions require companies to keep up with the times or go to the wall. Sometimes growth is necessary to cover overheads with falling margins; sometimes to compensate for the rise in wages; in other cases to buy larger units of machinery which enable cheaper production. In a vast number of cases the company will not be able, either financially, commercially or humanly, to grow rapidly enough by itself. In such cases, the need will arise naturally, by co-operation either to catch up with, or anticipate the expected growth of rival companies.

The concept of co-operation covers a multitude of situations. We must therefore first see what are the principal forms of co-operation.

FORMS OF CO-OPERATION

First, we must distinguish between partial and full co-operation. Partial co-operation can again be sub-divided into 'joint trading' and 'co-operation by agreement'.

1 In joint trading the partners each put part of their trade into a new business unit, which from then on will conduct that part of the business on joint account. Whether this new business unit should also assume the legal structure of a joint venture or whether it should be a limited company, a partnership or something else again depends on the situation. It is an obvious solution not only to improve a part of a company, but also for the joint undertaking of new activities.
2 In co-operation by agreement partners do not establish new business units but join forces in some field or other by means of a contract. Apart from combining sales activities in cartels (in countries where legislation permits), and co-operation in complementary product ranges, this form of co-operation can also be used in the case of mutual specialization.

Full co-operation can be achieved in two ways: acquisitions (or take-overs) and mergers. In the case of a take-over the control of a company is transferred to the management of another, sometimes as a result of negotiations, but frequently by way of a private or open bid for the shares. Apart from the interests of the companies concerned, the private financial positions of the shareholders frequently also play a part in these take-overs.

Full co-operation by means of a true merger is reached by the amalgamation of more or less equal firms. The legal forms of full co-operation are as numerous as they are complicated, and it is not necessary to detail them here.

CO-OPERATION AS AN AID TO DEVELOPMENT

In order to choose the right means of co-operation—and to answer the most important question of all, whether or not to co-operate—it is easier if, for the moment, we forget the forms of co-operation and consider the future development of the company, starting from its present position. Co-operation can only succeed if it aids the development of the company in a clearly definable way. Co-operation for other reasons will almost always end in disappointment. It is inevitably accompanied by problems, worries and costs; these must be compensated by the advantages any agreement offers to the partners. Otherwise, losses will accrue.

FUNCTIONS OF THE COMPANY

In a capitalist society the company has a vital role to play. Playing it badly spells ruin to the company, a ruin which is foreshadowed by a falling share of the market, by falling profits (or increasing losses) which finally end in a sell-out or liquidation. A company, to maintain its rights of survival, has to exercise three basic functions:

1 The *commercial* activity means searching for a supply of goods in order, by means of a production or distribution process, to bring them to the markets where there is a demand for them.
2 *Production* is the efficient use of labour, plant and equipment for manufacture and distribution.
3 *Research and development* means continually creating and improving products and methods.

A successful co-operation between firms always means that it is directed at strengthening one or more of these three functions of the partners. Such strengthening can only be achieved if co-operation is sought in the right direction.

DIRECTIONS OF CO-OPERATION

Co-operation can be sought either vertically or horizontally. We speak of vertical co-operation if a company seeks its partners from among suppliers or customers. Horizontal co-operation means a linking-up on the same level, i.e. with partners manufacturing the same or complementary products.

Clear thinking on co-operation must answer the following questions: which business functions are to be strengthened? In what direction should co-operation be sought? Which form(s) of co-operation could be considered?

There is a clear connection between the company's functions, the direction of co-operation, and the form which should be given to this co-operation. This connection is shown in the following plan: vertically we find the business functions at which co-operation may be aimed, horizontally the directions in which co-operation may be sought. In the twelve resulting squares we find the most suitable forms of co-operation for the function and direction concerned.

FULL OR PARTIAL CO-OPERATION

Full co-operation (a merger) is practically essential if *vertical* integration of the commercial function is desired: the supplying partner, in particular, would be irreparably harmed if the co-operation were to be terminated—which is always possible in partial co-operation. The same applies to *horizontal* integration of the *manufacturing* function—which, in any case, is only meaningful if the partners carry more or less the same range: here too one passes a point of no return. *Horizontal* integration of the *commercial* function where partners make the same products is generally inadvisable. If the partners do not, between them, completely dominate the market such agreements will always result in a loss of turnover which will soon exceed the savings in cost in the manufacturing function (see also pages 150–161). Forms of co-operation on a contract basis (price agreements, etc.) covering the entire branch of industry do not have this drawback. Co-operation in

	Vertical Co-operation		Horizontal Co-operation	
	with suppliers	with customers	same range of products	complementary range of products
Commercial	merger desirable	merger imperative	complete co-operation (merger) often highly dangerous; only agreements in various products acceptable	any form possible
Production	co-operative collaboration or co-operation on the basis of an agreement both good possibilities mergers preferable in a limited number of cases; particularly those with very high research and development costs			
Research and development	co-operation generally not very attractive		merger essential	mostly no point in co-operation

sales is also without risk: here mutual co-operation may well be successful.

Horizontal commercial co-operation where ranges are complementary may also be extremely successful in a co-operative form (see also pages 44–54). This form of combining is the most expansionary of all and is well suited to growing markets, as opposed to vertical co-operation which is usually more defensive in character.

Both vertically and horizontally, the research and development function is suitable for practical and co-operative collaboration, provided the results to which partners are entitled are properly determined beforehand.

WHETHER OR NOT TO CO-OPERATE

There has already been a warning against the risky forms of co-operation designed to serve purposes other than the real functions of a company. Even within the scope of these business functions, there are still many blank spaces, which must be regarded as warnings against rash business engagements; the number of the situations in which co-operation offers advantages is restricted.

But, apart from such hazards, we must emphasize that the risky road of co-operation should not be avoided if the development of the company requires it. The perspectives offered by successful co-operation cannot be attained in any other way and are certainly worth a few years of extra effort and anxiety.

A NEW FORM OF CO-OPERATION

The list offered by 'A bird's-eye view of co-operation' should be considered a modest catalogue of the various forms and conditions of co-operation. An important criterion for the grouping of kinds of co-operation—a criterion which does not emerge very clearly from this list—is the extent to which the owner/manager loses his independence and/or his say in the company. This is one of the main obstacles to mergers, and is one of the reasons why they are inadvisable unless absolutely imperative. There are, after all, many other possibilities. A partial restriction of independence is found, for example, in an endless variety of buying rings, research pooling, cartels, sole representations, etc.

At this point, details must be given of one form of co-operation which is of great importance. This comparatively new form, which ensures a large measure of independence, is best described as 'co-operation on complementary product ranges'. Partly due to the development of EEC, it is now becoming more general. What it does and does not include, in what circumstances it is to be recommended and how it should be brought about, is described below.

It seems probable that, as uniform legal systems come into being in EEC, this form of co-operation will only be possible for products which have a high added value and for which markets, by their very nature, will remain separate, in spite of the lifting of import restrictions.

Factors which help to maintain such a natural division of markets are: transport costs; differences in tastes, and different customs in regions with a different language and/or a different race. If these last two factors do not apply, it is obvious that co-operation on complementary product ranges may also develop into mergers. If the relative level of the added value should fall, it seems likely that co-operation on complementary product ranges will be replaced by 'joint ventures'.

CO-OPERATION ON COMPLEMENTARY PRODUCT RANGES; ASSOCIATION WITH INDEPENDENCE

AN IDEAL FOR MANY EUROPEAN BUSINESSMEN IN THE MEDIUM-SIZED FIRM

The medium-sized company in many European countries is still, on the whole, a family business with all the accompanying advantages and disadvantages. Fathers, sons and grandsons determine development; the company becomes an indivisible part of the family and the family is axiomatic to the firm. Not infrequently, great sacrifices are made to keep the company in the family. Speaking of 'the need for independence' in this case is a very poor description of the actual circumstances. It is the family relationship with the firm which explains the need for independence.

There is no doubt that the greatest obstacle to co-operation involving some degree of integration is the fear of losing independence. To many, co-operation still means a merger, and a merger is an amalgamation which cannot be undone: it is irrevocable.

The ideal for many businessmen in medium-sized firms is a form of co-operation in which they need not open the gates of their own companies. In other words, the link with the partner need be no closer than those with customers. A form of co-operation is desired which does not affect the rights of the individual company, yet leaves the businessman free to act as he wishes. This ideal—let us say at once—is unattainable. All forms of co-operation impose restrictions. Nevertheless, it is possible to reach agreements which allow partners to keep some degree of their independence. An important factor here is the measure of integration.

As long as co-operation is limited to one section of the business, the overall independence of the participating companies is hardly affected at all. The more parts of a company to be integrated, however, the more difficult it becomes to retain independence.

THE MAINTENANCE OF INDEPENDENCE IN CO-OPERATION

When considering the possibilities of maintaining independence in medium-sized firms, one must distinguish between the agreements which are co-operative and those where there is integration between constituent parts.

Among the collaborations which are co-operative are those agreements between companies where a relatively small part of the capital is set aside for a special purpose. Such forms of collaboration are found especially in commerce. In the fields of buying, export and home sales there are many combinations; some indeed have grown into enormous organizations. Almost every legal structure is used. In the fields of production and development examples are rarer, but they do exist. Only a very few instances are known of the common production of parts or of further manufacture; co-operation here is not so obvious. Such small quantities are generally required by any single firm that one would have to persuade large numbers to join in the venture. In that case, even if one were successful, the yield would be outweighed by the energy spent on the project. Furthermore, the manufacture of parts is often sub-contracted, because the company is not sure that the use of the part or even of the product will be continued. The product which is sub-contracted often requires a certain specialization which can only be gained after years of experience, and in that case, output by the company may be too small ever to obtain that experience. Frequently, too, the product itself is of a temporary nature, or the conditions of the supplier are such that in the larger firm the work could only be carried out at a much higher cost, or at the same cost but with less after-sales service. During recent years many 'joint ventures' have been formed where combinations, usually of national and foreign producers, establish and develop new production units.

In all these cases there is a restriction of independence which only applies to the specific object pursued with the portion of capital which has been set aside. One might say that, for all forms of co-operative collaboration or joint trading, the limitation of independence is purely quantitative, and in all cases clearly defined. This does not mean that, sometimes, large parts of the firm's independence will not disappear. In the Dutch food industry, for example, many participants have hardly any independence at all. Nevertheless, in these cases the nature of the independence has not altered; only the fields in which these companies were independent have gradually dwindled. In co-operations where the integration factor is predominant the consequences may be quite different. The possibilities of maintaining independence in co-operations of an integrative nature depend directly on the extent to which the realization of the economies or advantages result in the mixing of definite elements of the capital of partners.

If the co-operation is aimed at substantial economies by means of full integration of the production apparatus, combined with drastic moves of people and machines through a re-classification of the factories belonging to the participating companies—which in scale-increasing mergers is usually the case—then it is quite impossible for the original independence to be totally maintained. In these cases, a new firm is created in which none of the original functions is even recognizable, let alone demonstrable as such.

After a merger to increase the scale of manufacture, the independence of the individual businessman has not lessened—it has completely disappeared, unless he takes over the management of the new company. In that case his independence may be restricted by a proportional change in the ownership of shares; it is, however, essentially unimpaired. The entrepreneur who, after a merger, has to share the management of a company with others or accept the leadership of others, encounters situations which are completely new to him and which—if he has long been used to independence— he is often unable to accept.

In a merger, considerable demands are made on personal co-operation. The new situation also requires new, adapted personalities. This is one of the reasons why some top executives are completely submerged by the new organization after a merger, whereas others develop to a surprising extent. This, too, is an aspect of independence; one has to face every problem that comes along, but one is never able to cope equally with all these problems. Co-operation therefore may sometimes complement the weaker spots of individual entrepreneurship.

CO-OPERATION ON COMPLEMENTARY PRODUCT RANGES WITH FOREIGN FIRMS

To find solutions to avoid the disadvantages both of a superficial collaboration and a freedom-depriving co-operation, is usually very difficult, if not impossible. But a special form of agreement, where this can be achieved, is the co-operation on complementary product ranges with foreign firms.

The purpose of this kind of co-operation is to enlarge the range of each of the partners without increasing the development costs of either of them. Integration is limited to the formation of the product range—the companies, their production apparatus, their administration and sales departments remain as separate as they were before.

Why should this kind of co-operation make sense, especially with foreign partners? Every firm has its own appearance in the home market, its own image (see also pages 152–153). Combining the ranges of two companies within the same country, operating on the same market, with the same, or almost the same, group of consumers, does not offer much chance of an increased turnover. The consumer is acquainted with both firms, more or less knows their strong and weak points, and is called on by representatives of both these companies. A combination in this case is a disadvantage to the consumer: he has less choice and fewer possibilities for negotiations. He will, therefore, be inclined to seek compensation from a different company altogether, so that, in the end, the combined partner companies would be the losers! For a combination across frontiers, however, this does not apply. Even if both firms have an export department, they usually cover only small parts of the foreign market. There are opportunities abroad, but these are almost always less than those of the manufacturer who is thoroughly at home in the area and with the consumers in that region.

A Dutch firm exporting to the UK generally has no clear image there. It can only expect to succeed if it builds up an organization which is comparable to the selling apparatus of a UK concern in the same line. But such an organization is extremely costly, especially where tariff barriers already make the imported product dearer in the first place.

Conditions are changing, and we continually see foreign manufacturers entering our markets and building up their own sales organizations here—although not always successfully. It is still true that the better one knows a market, the better one can organize its operation. A sales method which is successful in North America may fail completely in Europe, and vice versa. During the past few years, several complacent non-European companies have learnt this the hard way. In due course there will effectively be one market for the whole of the EEC. Despite this, however, every new market will present new problems. Creating an image—the only guarantee for a continuity in turnover—will require time and, therefore, money.

Many European companies, will, however, have to make such investment, as they will also be under attack on their home markets. The only defence against intruders on the home market is to be better, to be more varied, to offer more service; in short, to raise the entire range of sale-determining factors to a higher level. This too will cost money. Obviously, enormous amounts could be saved and much effort avoided if companies from different sales areas could develop their exports by including each other's range of products in their own sales department thus avoiding the development costs of individually widening their range.

As will be shown further on, this form of co-operation does not, particularly during the first few years, affect the independence of the individual entrepreneur. He can determine, step-by-step, to what extent he is willing to surrender parts of his independence. In all these cases, he will have a better understanding of what he is surrendering and what he may expect in return, than he would in the case of an outright merger.

CO-OPERATION ON COMPLEMENTARY PRODUCT
RANGES: SUITABLE COMPANIES

Co-operation on complementary product ranges is not always the indicated solution. In general, it is suitable for the following types of business:

1 Those which, because of their size or their commercial tradition, do not cover the entire range of a particular product in price, quality, raw materials used, packaging, service, etc. One might say that any company that could, with the same sales department and the same effort, include more articles in its range, qualifies for this type of co-operation. It is limited by the maximum number of articles any representative can carry, without the sales potential of one of his products diminishing. The number varies according to the type of article and the sales method. If the range is too wide, full justice cannot be done to any single article.

2 Firms whose strength is not so much the efficiency of their production apparatus, as the exclusivity and the specific properties of their products. As a rule, concerns specializing in mass production and the lowest possible costs are therefore not so suitable. If the advantages of co-operation are to come from economizing on production costs, a merger is a far more obvious solution than co-operation on complementary product ranges.

3 Companies which, in their own market with their traditional range, can obtain only a limited share of the market and for which a development of a complementary range of their own is not profitable.

4 Companies which have (or threaten to have) an 'optimum' production far surpassing the possible turnover (the potential) of their home market, e.g. because of the Common Market, as the home market becomes increasingly less protected.

ADVANTAGES AND RISKS OF CO-OPERATION ON
COMPLEMENTARY PRODUCT RANGES

In order to consider all the effects of this type of co-operation with a foreign partner the operational area of a company must be divided into three parts: 1 The home market of the company involved. 2 Exports to partner's home market. 3 The market which for both firms is the export market.

1 If the present consumers on the home market are approached with the combined ranges, we may expect the total turnover of both ranges to increase. Compared to previous periods, however, the home company's turnover will have dropped (see Figure 1). This fall will, in general, be greater the more the range is integrated. The fall in the home company's production will increase the fixed costs per unit.

The commission earned from the turnover of imported products will not entirely compensate the loss on the home company's production. In general, the margin of profit on import commissions is so much less than the profit on home manufactures, that the turnover of imported production is hardly ever sufficient to compensate the entire loss. The

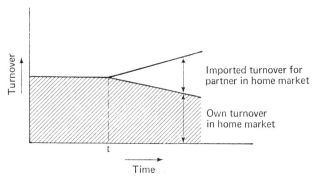

Fig. 1. Influence of co-operation on home market.

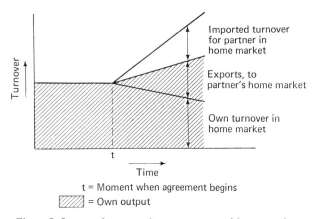

Fig. 2. Influence of co-operation on exports and home market.

advantage of the co-operation must be derived from the exports (see Figure 2).

2 In the partner's home market, the export sales of the firm will form the direct opposite of the import sales discussed above. In the home country, the total turnover will also increase, but here it is the partner's own sales which will lose a little to the home country's exports (i.e. his imports). Here too, this effect will probably be more marked as the ranges are presented more as one whole. One must realize that large exports are essential if co-operation is to be a success, for these exports have a double obligation: firstly, they must reduce the increased fixed costs per product unit (caused by the fall in the

home turnover) to the original level or less. Secondly, they must compensate for the fall in the margin of profit which always occurs in exports.

3 Additional turnover may be obtained by a combined penetration of markets which are new to both firms. The great advantage of co-operation here lies in the availability of a wide range, and in the distribution of the high initial costs over more than one company. Quite often, it is more advantageous to seek another partner in the new market together, so that the entire exchange procedure may be repeated. Finally, if both firms have been exporting to a certain country for some time, they may be able to strengthen their exports by telescoping the two export organizations and keeping only the best agents of each to work with the entire range.

Strangely enough, the *risk* of exchanging complementary product ranges with foreign companies is that of too rapid development of the agreement rather than that of failure, for failure causes far less harm here than it does in practically any other kind of co-operation: here the agreement can be unravelled fairly easily.

If, however, the exported range is really successful in the partner's market, increased production may be required from the factory which cannot be realized with the existing plant, if quality and times of delivery are to be maintained. Exports may become explosive, all the more so if the foreign markets are thoroughly explored, and if the potential is larger there than it is on the home market. A combination not with one, but with various partners at the same time, may produce the same effect.

There is another, longer-term risk. Each firm will sell products of its partners from abroad under its own flag. The images of the partner companies, which are shown by their entire attitude as producer, trader, financier, etc., are not known to their fellow partners, and will only become known as orders are carried out. Only then will seller and customer be able to see, for instance, that the finish is not all it should be, that colour fastness is not up to expectation, that delivery times are not strictly adhered to, complaints are not dealt with satisfactorily, the administrative side is somewhat careless: in fact, all the strong and weak sides of the factors by which the customer measures and classifies the supplier.

Care will have to be taken that customers do not identify the

weak points of the partners with the home firm. It takes more time
to establish a good name than it does to destroy one.

In this form of co-operation, therefore, there are potential forces
which may cause considerable changes in a company's operations,
particularly if one takes into account the changes caused by the
Common Market. These alterations offer advantages but also
involve considerable risks.

RESTRICTING THE RISKS

If one can succeed in avoiding the risks, great possibilities will open
up, especially in the Common Market. This kind of agreement is
particularly suited to the regional firm in Europe. A co-operation
of complementary product ranges will, on the one hand, enable a
company to retain the advantages of a strong regional position
and, on the other—at the same time—to achieve an international
spread of interests and an increase in turnover which it could never
realize by itself within the same time-span.

In general, one may say that caution is the main requirement, if
the risks inherent in co-operation are to be limited. One must not
try to achieve too much within too short a time. For preference,
the tempo should be adjustable; one must be able to delay and
accelerate, and if necessary even take a step backwards. In order to
develop the combination into more than just a simple temporary
exchange of products, and to achieve a balanced growth towards a
continued co-operation, the following points must be borne in mind:

 I UNIFORM ANALYSIS The better one is able to forecast
 developments in the various products in the combined sales,
 the smaller will be the inherent risks. Also, the sooner one will
 be able to intensify the agreement and benefit from the advantages it brings. A good analysis will in the first place, supply
 a complete and comparable picture of the precise business of
 the partners in the combination, the weak and the strong
 aspects of the various component parts, etc. From this one can
 see more clearly in what direction(s) the agreement should be
 developed. Secondly, the analysis should give forecasts for a
 first phase, as this phase might require alternative means of
 regulation. In this way recommendations can be evolved for
 arrangements during the first phase and for an administrative

system which will enable those involved in the co-operation to keep track of developments, make timely intervention possible and arm themselves against all possible risks.

2 PHASING A division into phases is one of the best means of ensuring the success of the agreement. Attention can be paid to every single step, and each step can be so regulated that the consequences remain calculable. These phases should not include more than can be kept strictly in hand. Generally, such a division into phases will include moments at which a link or a further link must be defined in a formal regulation.

During the first phase, ties should be kept as loose as possible. The quantities which the companies are to sell for one another will be limited, sales ranges will only contain parts of the factory ranges, customers called on with the partner's ranges will only form a small part of the total potential of customers in their own area. The end of the first phase—which may last for several years—is marked by a lifting of the restrictions regarding quantity, product range and the customers visited.

Critical moments during the later phases will be:

(a) The exchange of production.
(b) Common calculation and specialization in production.
(c) The pooling of profits and joint ventures in export countries.

The duration of phases may vary greatly. Initially, it is advisable to restrict a phase to the period between the moments at which each new product or range is put on the market. As time goes on, if the co-operation continues, the periods covered by the arrangements will lengthen. A sound development will ultimately result in a contract-for-life between the companies.

3 ARRANGEMENTS For every phase in the co-operation, or for each extension of it, a new arrangement could be drawn up. It has, however, proved wiser to make an extensive analysis of the co-operation process before drawing up the first agreement. If the co-operation process is analysed into separate elements from beginning to end, and alternative arrangements have been set out for each element, an instrument is created whereby arrangements can be studied and discussed simply and clearly, and which also shows all partners the significance and the

consequences of the agreements. It is then possible, as it were, to programme agreements.

A complete analysis of such a co-operation process into elements, with the possible alternatives for each, would carry us beyond the scope of this section. It would cover the development and exhibition of production ranges, the building up of sales ranges, the actual sales, up to and including production and administration. The number of possible arrangements is enormous, far greater than one might think at first sight. The main advantage of this method is that one can rapidly reach clear and unequivocal agreements.

Although companies must have a common perspective, it is wise never to arrange more than one phase, i.e. the next, in detail. In these arrangements the risks must be limited. Arrangements must be drawn up and signed, and if necessary worked out legally with the agreement of purpose clearly shown. If this agreement of purpose did not exist, one might be led to think one was going to realize a phase which in fact, was not realizable. A signed arrangement forces partners to consider consequences beforehand and this eliminates many problems which may arise during the collaboration.

CONCLUSION

For many medium-sized firms, the co-operation on complementary product ranges with foreign companies offers opportunities which will enable them to grow to the size required for future markets in Europe. Superficial ideas about the arrangement of a co-operation will inevitably lead to disappointment. If each phase is well-prepared and arranged, then risks will be reduced to a minimum.

If a type of company is suitable for this kind of agreement, the possibilities, given an equal amount of effort, are greater than those offered by any kind of co-operative collaboration, *and* they can be realized without big investments. Compared to integrative co-operation, such as mergers, the possibilities of economizing and the rate of growth may be less, but at least one knows step-by-step what one wins and what one relinquishes, while the independence and character of the company are retained.

4 Mergers

THE CHOICE OF PARTNER

A merger is the most far-reaching form of co-operation. In contrast to any other kind of association, including take-overs, a merger demands the planning and realization of a completely new business policy at the most difficult moments, i.e. during the preparations and at the point of realization of the co-operation itself.

Leaving aside irresponsible adventures, all other kinds of co-operation are dictated by a business policy which originated from some kind of development investigation and which was drawn up beforehand. In mergers, the development investigation takes place during negotiations and during the first two years of the merger. The talks consist mainly of development investigation.

The exceptional position of mergers arises from the equality of the partners. All the development policy practised, either consciously or unconsciously, in the partner firms must be revised and adapted. None of the partners can expect that the development policy which, in their own company, provided the reasons for considering a merger, will determine the policy of the new concern after the merger.

This completely open and, therefore, also uncertain and risky situation makes the choice of partners with whom one may seriously consider the possibility of a merger, of vital importance.

The section immediately below, deals mainly with the problem of choosing a partner. Here again the development investigation in one's own company is a considerable help in the first steps towards a merger, even though, in this case, it is certain that the conclusions reached will, in the merger talks, have to be radically adapted to the interests of the partners. Many of the cases cited below show that the choice of the right partner is all-important in ensuring success for the merger.

THE WAY TO A MERGER FOR THE MEDIUM-SIZED COMPANY

INTRODUCTION

It has been said that the increasing number of mergers during the past few years has been the result of a general inclination towards collaboration, rather than of a direct aim towards reducing cost-prices. On the other hand, some reputable authorities consider that a concentration of companies at the present time is 'in the nature of things'. On considering the matter from the outside—or, if one prefers, from above—one reaches similar conclusions. If, however, we put ourselves in the place of the businessman, we think he would do well to realize that the only merger which will be successful is one which leads to a definite improvement in business results.

In big concerns, where acquisitions of medium-sized companies regularly take place by means of share exchanges, the development of the acquired companies is gradually adapted to the general policy of the parent. Those concerned can usually deduce the purposes of such mergers quite clearly from existing policy and growth trends. It is, however, extremely difficult for medium-sized companies to compare their policies with the directed concentration of power of the big enterprises, for a merger of equal medium-sized firms obviously cannot build on an existing policy. For management, the merger means a suddenly increased scale of all problems by at least 2:1, combined with the building up of a completely new development policy from the carefully balanced interests of the existing companies.

Apart from problems of power, influential shareholder positions and psychological barriers, the right choice of partners in this case is therefore a major problem. For lack of better criteria, the choice of partners in mergers of medium-sized companies is often a matter of coincidence, such as being situated in the same area, a casual meeting of managers in a business or non-business connection, family relationships, a director who is on the board of both companies, banking connections, etc.

Many of these hopefully begun, but more or less incidental, contacts have—sometimes after years of difficult negotiations—resulted in deep disappointment. Such disappointments raise the question of whether the problem of a merger should be approached more systematically. This can be done, and there follows an indication of how to develop the main lines along which equal medium-sized companies might progress towards a merger in a more systematic way.

For the medium-sized concern, the road to a merger is divided into two stages. During the first stage, by means of an analysis of the position of the firm, a programme of requirements is drawn up, which must be met by a possible partner. During the second stage, an attempt is made on the basis of this programme to find a partner with whom to start effective, rapid and successful negotiations.

THE TOTAL INTERESTS OF THE COMPANY

The starting-point must be the interest of the firm as a whole. This may seem rather obvious, but one must remember that there may be enormous differences between the interests of the entire company and the interests of a group within or surrounding it. Take for example, the shareholders; they may, for good reasons, put a brake on the rate of expansion; they may be anxious to have none of their rights curtailed or they may object to investments which could keep down the dividend on their shares. In other cases, they may tend to favour excessive expansion—possibly with, possibly without, a merger—in the hope of obtaining more marketable stock, or because the chance of growth and the security of shares in a large company is higher than in a (frequently private) family firm.

If the special interests of groups in or around the company are taken into account during the first stage of the merger talks, there is a risk that the issue will become confused. Possibilities which are equally important to the shareholders may not be explored, or shareholders may be pushed in a direction which is not to their advantage. The interests of shareholders, and equally the interests of the board of directors, of managing directors, employees and customers must all be considered separately.

FIRST STAGE: ANALYSIS OF ONE'S OWN COMPANY

INVESTIGATION

A merger is effective only if the results obtained by the company—particularly over the long-term—improve demonstrably, e.g. in:

1 Higher returns on the invested capital, measured according to actual dividends.
2 A higher income for all full-time employees.
3 A higher percentage of own financing.

Improved results can only be expected if a merger opens up definite possibilities for a marked improvement in one or more of the main business functions:

1 Trading.
2 Research and development.
3 Production.

The proposed investigation will consist of one or more of the directors, aided as necessary by one or more specialists systematically analysing each of these functions. Does the company lag behind its competitors? What new developments are to be expected in technology and on the market in the near future? And finally, how could the partner in a merger strengthen the group in a way which cannot within a reasonable period be realized by the company acting alone?

The point of the investigation is to analyse systematically the available knowledge of the industry or sector of industry and the spirit of enterprise in the company. We shall now proceed to deal further with these main functions; the twenty-two examples included, have been derived partly from experience, partly from other literature on the subject.

TRADING FUNCTION

The trading function dominates the incoming and outgoing flow of capital funds and products, and aims at directing these streams—via development and production—from the place of greatest supply to the place of greatest demand. Here for the first time we encounter *financing*. A merger may, in various ways, increase the flow of financial means to the firm.

Case A The merger of three companies so increased the subscribed capital that a quotation on the Stock Exchange became possible. The result was more marketable shares and better opportunities for financing.

Case B The bank credits of three firms could be converted into a debenture loan.

Case C Two companies gained such strength by merging that they were able to persuade a series of smaller companies to join the merger, without themselves losing any of their power.

Another aspect of the trading function is *buying*. It is clear that an increase in the size of the company will enhance its position towards suppliers.

Case D Three bicycle factories were able, by a merger, to standardize various parts and buy them at considerably lower prices.

By increasing the size of the company, some links in the buying process can often be eliminated.

Case E After the merger of several woollen mills, it was found the new concern could, at its own risk, buy wool direct on the world market.

Sometimes firms also find themselves big enough to manufacture parts which, up till then, they had to buy.

Case F After the merger of several appliance manufacturers, the new group was able to set up its own company for plastics components.

A third trading function is *selling*. A merger can strengthen sales in many ways. For instance, it may be desirable to increase the market share of a certain article.

Case G A furniture manufacturer wished to push his furniture in the medium price range under a brand name and looked for a partner in order together to obtain the market share required for these goods.

Case H A wool manufacturer merged with a similar foreign company in order to develop a collection of patterns together twice a year.

One may imagine the entire market of a product as being divided into market areas and sales channels. By a merger it is possible to add a complementary area or channel to this sales range.

Case I A merger of two textile mills made it possible to combine sales via wholesalers and sales via the retail trade.

Case J A domestic appliance manufacturer covering forty per cent of the exports of a certain article but only ten per cent of the home market, sought the partnership of a company with a large share of the home market but small export results.

To lessen seasonal influences or trend risks it may be most important to widen a company's range.

Case K A shoe factory with seventy per cent of its sales in the high price range looked for co-operation with a company manufacturing mainly cheaper shoes.

Most groups of consumers have a series of requirements, and the average company meets only part of these. It may be very profitable for a firm to serve its customers more widely by adding a complementary range to its own.

Case L By co-operating with an insurance company, a life assurance company was able to increase its business with the same number of inspectors and at the same time to improve service to its customers (the middlemen).

Finally, if a company reaches a certain size some links in the sales process may be eliminated.

Case M The merger of a number of engineering works resulted in the establishment of one export organization for EEC countries and another for all other exports.

RESEARCH AND DEVELOPMENT

The research and development function deals with the creation of new products and production methods. New technical possibilities must constantly be explored with a keen eye to the market. 'R and D' is often the soul of a company; but it demands enormous cost and effort. A merger may quite often divide this load over several shoulders, while more benefit can be derived from the effects of the development.

The first possibility is that two companies, each with its own technical speciality, should merge in order to make a spectacular new product.

Case N The merger of a manufacturer of steel window-frames and doors and a plastics manufacturer led to the use of plastics in window-frames.

It may also be wise to look for a partner possessing important patents.

Case O The merger of a big iron-foundry and a smaller one which had done important research work on the manufacture of heat-proof materials.

Lastly, mergers aimed at improving research may also be very successful.

Case P A factory for the manufacturer of household appliances sought a partner manufacturing technical refrigerating plants in order to develop together new systems for domestic refrigerators.

PRODUCTION FUNCTION

The results gained by a merger in production processes are drawing more and more attention. A merger in this function may mean two forms of progress: in production technique and in production control.

In *production technique,* the following developments are possible. If one succeeds in enlarging the production series the fixed cost per unit will drop.

Case Q In a merger of automobile factories, the styling and tooling costs could—by introducing common car-body models—be spread over a larger number of units.

By means of a merger, it is often possible to use new and profitable production methods requiring bigger investments.

Case R A merger of a number of engineering works brought about the establishment of one central profitable production unit for automatic machinery.

Seasonal influences on the full employment of machines may sometimes be greatly limited by a merger.

Case S After the merger of two cotton-mills the new company attained a ten per cent higher machine output because the firms had their seasonal peaks at different periods.

Finally, nowadays, there are also mergers in which one of the partners solves part of the personnel problems of the other.

Case T A bicycle factory selling more than it can produce in the present labour situation merged with another which had a capacity surplus.

Production control offers many new possibilities to the enlarged company. For instance, specialized departments may be established.

Case U After the merger of two food manufacturers, one of the first decisions was to form a department for quality control on the basis of available statistics.

More attention can also be paid to administrative procedures.

Case V After the merger of three brick-works, the new company was able to make the mechanization of the order and delivery planning pay its way. This had not been possible for the companies separately.

INVESTIGATION INTO QUALITY AND QUANTITY

The main principle in this part of the investigation is contained in the German proverb: '*In der Beschränkung zeigt sich der Meister*' (Quality reveals itself in restraint). In the first place, it is advisable for the investigation to be limited to the subjects mentioned earlier (see pages 58–62)—financing, buying, development, production technique and production control.

The first step in the investigation is to form a rough picture of the quality requirements which a merger partner must meet to offer advantages which cannot be obtained in any other way. With the help of the experience and knowledge available in the firm, these requirements can be set down in the same way as the examples detailed above. This is the main part of the investigation, for considerations overlooked now will not have a chance at a later stage, and items which are thoughtlessly set down now will, at a later stage, cause confusion and disorder. On the other hand, excessive detail must be avoided, as this might easily become a kind of general X-ray of the company, which, although no doubt useful, would take more time than the management can spare.

The second step is to define these rough requirements, which are still somewhat speculative, by means of a quantitative approach. Even more important is a considered estimate of the periods within which new markets must be acquired, new products developed, new production techniques introduced in order to enable the company to continue its main functions successfully.

Here too, one must keep to the main outlines and not get bogged down in a morass of figures. This presents special problems, for in order to group the figures to form a clear picture, the sub-division of those units in which the situation is defined is of the utmost importance. This applies equally to the division of plant into groups of machines, the division of the year into periods and a host of similar problems. Bearing in mind that it will later be desirable to obtain comparable figures from the possible partner in a merger, it is clear that the heart of this investigation stage is '*l'art de grouper les chiffres*' (the ability to combine numbers).

Apart from a clear list of the requirements which a partner should meet, the quantitative approach also presents a good picture of the arguments which can be made for or against a merger. Now that this picture has emerged, the moment has come to see whether a merger will present advantages or disadvantages to sections of the company which differ from the arguments applying to the group as a whole. Given such a clear picture of the direction a merger will take, this should present no very great difficulties.

SECOND STAGE: IN SEARCH OF A MERGER PARTNER

FRANKNESS: A PROBLEM

The second stage of the investigation begins the moment it is clear what the company as a whole, and the special groups of interests, expect from a merger. Here one is faced with the task not only of making a list of all the companies which could be considered as a partner, but also with the problem of how to obtain sufficient data on these companies to make a decision. The prevailing ideas on the secrecy of business data make this extremely complicated. On this point a comparison with conditions in the United States is very illuminating. We shall, therefore, refer more than once to a study by the American specialist on mergers, G. D. McCarthy (see McCarthy, George D., 'Premeditated Merger', *Harvard Business Review*, January/February, 1961).

Frankness in matters of finance, products, turnover and other vital business data, which in American enterprise is considered usual, not infrequently seems to the British to be a kind of obnoxious exhibitionism. There is an unwillingness to allow the outsider a glimpse of the details of a company and it is therefore extremely difficult to obtain data on companies with which one is not already in direct contact. One may not, however, stop short at this negative conclusion. The danger of failure if choice is restricted to the companies within this circle, is too great. All available sources of information must be used, so as to include as many suitable companies as possible in the investigation.

THE ACQUISITION COMMITTEE

During the first phase of the merger investigation, the role of the board of directors is as a whole to advise, and even sometimes to take the initiative. The responsibility, however, is clearly on the executive management and during the quantitative approach shifts somewhat to the specialized executives. The present stage of the investigation—the choice of a partner, is a matter for board and management together. Here we have a subject where a capable member of the board will have a chance to justify a job which, of recent years, has given rise to so many theoretical discussions.

McCarthy wishes to entrust this part of the investigation to an 'acquisition committee', the composition of which would depend on the size of the company, the extent and intricacy of the merger programme, the different interests concerned and the time the members of the committee can devote to this work. He also makes the point that, in the case of opposed interests, an outsider on this committee may prove very useful. Although in America the company is regarded much more as a saleable object and emotional ties with the company play a smaller part than they do in the European medium-sized enterprise (frequently a family business), it seems reasonable that the choice of a partner for a merger should not be a job for the entire board of directors and the management. A small committee of directors and managers, with the possible addition of an outsider, will be able to make more rapid and effective progress.

SOURCES OF INFORMATION

The available sources of information differ greatly in value.

1 ADVERTISEMENTS Periodicals or newspapers carry advertisements asking or offering firms for sale. The chances of finding a suitable partner in this way are remote.

2 INFORMATION SERVICES Unlike in the United States, the information from these bureaux is meant for very different problems and is therefore of little use for our purpose. This information mainly concerns very small companies and generally only relates to capital and credit.

3 EMPLOYERS' ASSOCIATION At this stage of the investigation, now that there is a programme of requirements for a partner, a list of possible companies can sometimes be obtained from these associations. As a first, rough selection method the employers' organizations are therefore useful.

4 BANKS Recently, both big and merchant banks have become very conscious of the part they can play as an intermediary between companies. Quite often a bank fills the position of trusted adviser to a company, and banks also have a good deal of information concerning those companies, which are their customers.

5 BOARDS OF DIRECTORS Knowledge of companies obtained via the directors goes much deeper than information obtained through banks, but the number of companies with which they are in touch, or could easily come into contact, is smaller.

6 THE COMPANY'S OWN MANAGEMENT AND HEADS OF DEPARTMENTS It is a very good thing if, not only the board, but also the top executives of the company know of the plans

for a merger. Often, this group has wide and varied contacts in the business world, and, especially on the commercial side, may have valuable suggestions to make.

INFORMATION REQUIRED

Once the acquisition committee has found a number of potential partners it must obtain information on these companies which will enable it to make a choice. McCarthy uses a check-list of questions, a list which in itself presents an interesting picture of the ease with which data on other companies are obtained in America. Necessary information includes the balance-sheets and profit and loss acounts over a number of years, the proportional ownership of share capital, the production capacity and the principal items of machinery, employment of plant, labour contracts; attitude, age and years of service of executives and structure of their income, annual turnover of principal products, main sales channels and customers, and finally all data required to interpret these figures, such as valuation of stocks, depreciation policy, current obligations and probable developments.

This wonderful array of information to us in Europe, is generally unobtainable in such a complete form. However, thorough use of the sources mentioned above may still yield us far more data than is often thought possible.

EFFECT

If we say that to draw up qualitative requirements for a partner is the most essential, and quantifying these requirements the most difficult part of our investigation, then we must add that looking for and choosing potential partners, just because of the secrecy which surrounds vital business information in Europe, is the most absorbing and surprising stage of the road to a merger.

Once this stage has been completed we shall have not only the certainty that we have chosen the best out of all the possible alternatives, but we shall also find that, instead of the endless negotiations which so often precede a merger, we can now have businesslike and effective talks which—because they are founded on clearly defined expectations—offer the best chances coupled with the smallest risks.

THE MERGER AS A PROJECT

INTRODUCTION

Anyone who has ever helped to carry through a merger, will remember this period as a stormy time with congested diaries, numerous and often emotional discussions and great anxiety on how, out of the mass of changes and alterations, plain order and clear management will ever again emerge. And everyone who has seen a merger fail, will know how well-founded is this anxiety and how many dangers there are threatening the young concern.

A well-planned merger offers tremendous opportunities for the development of the man and the company, but these opportunities can only be won in a tough fight with stubborn material; a fight which will certainly require very great—often personal—sacrifice, years of hard work and resilience in face of disappointments.

Fortunately, the interests served by a good merger are well worth the trouble, and the satisfaction felt when the new concern finally develops its full power is an experience reserved exclusively for those who succeed in a big undertaking.

In mergers, the heart of the problem is that, with the manpower attuned only to cope with the normal straightforward development of the company, three matters must be dealt with at once within a short period:

1 The formulation of a new integrated company policy.
2 All the once-only regulations called for by a merger must be drawn up and put into operation.
3 The daily management of the companies must be kept more firmly in hand than ever.

Even if, by the right choice of partner and a method of negotiation which is entirely directed at the future common interest, the chief psychological barriers have been broken down, an extremely efficient planning of the merger process is still required to prevent a deadlock in the merger talks or—even worse—in the daily management. It is therefore essential that agreement is reached in the very early stages of negotiation on all the merger activities required and the connection between these activities. Only then can it be decided who will undertake the various operations and when they should be completed.

Here we have found the system of network planning which is usual for big projects nowadays, very useful. We have included such a network plan for a merger with extensive explanations of the various activities (see Figure 3). Naturally, this is only a generalized plan. Its use is dealt with in the merger activity described in the plan itself as Activity 2–3: 'Deciding on the merger approach'. At that point the plan for a definite case can be drawn up and used as a guide.

The plan has been included not only because of its network form. It embodies two essential aspects of the merger process: balance and co-ordination: If mergers fail, this is often because a disproportionate amount of attention has been concentrated on one comparatively small aspect. This may have been the company's legal structure, or production rationalization, the structure of top management or commercial innovations. The new concern will bear the scars of such one-sided attention and it will be sheer luck if such a merger succeeds. A second danger is the lack of coherence between the various activities. 'In-groups' may develop which go their own way without supervision. In this case the concern will not only bear scars—it will have become a many-headed monstrosity.

Realizing that no two mergers are the same, and that every merger really requires an individual approach, this plan includes those factors which all mergers have in common, and show the content and links between these factors. The auditor, tax expert, lawyer, solicitor or actuary will be able on each specific point to indicate more precisely what should be done in each separate case. The aim has been to give the broad outlines of the various activities; the plan shows the connection between them.

For the technical development, especially the planning of starting and completion dates, refer to the time-planning and the further delineation of the critical path in the network set out on pages 125–128.

NETWORK PLAN OF A MERGER

The plan is built up from a number of activities. In the following pages the contents of each activity are described; whenever possible these contents have been formulated as a job instruction. The beginning and final points of each activity have also been indicated. These have been described as the conditions required to open an activity or to regard it as completed. The end of one activity is the beginning of the next.

The beginning and end of each activity are numbered in such a way that the sequence of the intervening activities is indicated. Each activity is indicated by the numbers referring to its beginning and final point.

All the numbers have been indicated on the plan (see Figure 3). The lines show the sequence of activities. In the text the activities have been described in order of sequence, mentioning the beginning and final point of each.

Whenever necessary there is a reference to the comments on pages 118–124.

Financial-Legal Unification: Phases 1–20 (*see Comment* 1 *page* 118)

ACTIVITY 1–2

Minimum period: 1 month
Maximum period: 18 months

STARTING POINT: FUNDAMENTAL WILLINGNESS TO
NEGOTIATE

When businessmen are discussing co-operation there is always a moment when the idea of a merger is suggested and is no longer rejected by a number of those concerned with the arrangement. A group has then been formed which is willing to negotiate; once this group begins to meet more or less regularly, the moment of acceptance of the concept has passed. At this stage we may assume the merger process has begun.

PRELIMINARY CONSULTATIONS

This is the time when contacts are carefully scrutinized—when businessmen sound out one another, suggest possibilities, express wishes, etc. Positions are explored and determined; the advantages and disadvantages of amalgamation are roughly estimated and discussed; the limits of possible collaboration are fixed. During these talks some partners will gradually become more attracted by the idea of co-operation—others may wish to step out at this stage.

Pre-conditions are often made at this stage, e.g. a party may demand that the entire management of a company be accepted, or that a merger is not acceptable unless certain articles or brands will continue to be produced after the merger. Sometimes one side may demand that—no matter what the valuation of the companies may be—authority will, in any case, be divided on a 50–50 basis. One of the parties may also state that it will not be able to provide any additional funds that might be required to adjust the balance of capital. A decreasing interest of partners or certain preliminary conditions which are unacceptable to others may cause the merger talks to fail.

CONCLUDING POINT: FUNDAMENTAL WILLINGNESS
TO MERGE

If the talks do not fail, the moment will gradually be reached at which some, and sometimes all, of the partners will declare themselves willing in principle to embark on some kind of merger. They now wish to determine the conditions on which an amalgamation should be based.

See Comment 2.

ACTIVITY 2–3

Minimum period: 1 day
Maximum period: 1 month

STARTING POINT: FUNDAMENTAL WILLINGNESS TO MERGE

GETTING TO GRIPS WITH THE MERGER

After the preliminary talks it is necessary to make an inventory of the activities which must be undertaken with a view to the establishment of a merger. The inventory may be drawn up in various ways.

The most simple method is to discuss what activities should be undertaken and write them down. Later a report can be drawn up of the matters discussed during the various talks. Another method is the use of check-lists (viz, see pages 35–37). One can also make use of planning schemes. The most effective method of planning is to draw up a network of the activities which must be undertaken in the way shown in this chapter.

It should be added that, at this stage, no data are exchanged, although it is gradually becoming clear what data will have to be exchanged at a later date.

CONCLUDING POINT: FUNDAMENTAL WILLINGNESS TO
INVESTIGATE

When it has become clear which activities must be undertaken, the moment has come when there is a willingness to make the data necessary for these activities available either to the partners or to experts.

See Comment 3.

ACTIVITY 3–4

Minimum period: 1 month
Maximum period: 3 months

STARTING POINT: FUNDAMENTAL WILLINGNESS TO
INVESTIGATE

INVESTIGATING THE PURPOSES OF THE MERGER

At this stage investigations are made to obtain a (rough) idea of the
advantages which must be realized in the different business functions,
the risks, possible disadvantages, etc. Groups of managers, experts
or a combination of both are formed which are entrusted with parts
of these investigations.

The importance of the functions may vary according to the
business or combination of businesses. The depth of the investigations will therefore also vary considerably as to merger and function.
(Compare, for instance, a merger between insurance firms and a
merger between food manufacturers.)

The investigations must result in an exploration of each area of
the business:

1 PRODUCTION. Points to be discussed may include:

(a) A comparison of products, production apparatus and
    production methods.
(b) The division of labour, plant and surface space in the
    departments of the various companies.
(c) An examination of the relative position of each company
    in its sector of industry and that of the total number of
    companies in the sector.
(d) An examination of the production technique in the partner
    companies in comparison to that in other concerns at
    home and abroad, etc.

2 SALES:

(a) A comparative examination of products and product
    development.

(b) An estimate of competitors and the determination of
relative market positions.

(c) An examination of the images of the companies, etc.

3 RESEARCH AND DEVELOPMENT. A comparative examination of product development and research in the partner firms
and their relative position in this respect as regards other
companies at home and abroad.

Sometimes the financial positions, or other aspects which
may be relevant in special cases, will also have to be considered.

CONCLUDING POINT: UNDERSTANDING OF THE
ADVANTAGES AND DISADVANTAGES OF A MERGER IN
REGARD TO EACH BUSINESS FUNCTION

This is the moment at which the companies know where they
stand in regard to each essential function. The partners have got a
clear picture of what can be obtained by a merger and what could
not be attained without it.

See Comment 4.

ACTIVITY 4-5

Minimum period: 1 month
Maximum period: 4 months

STARTING POINT: UNDERSTANDING OF ADVANTAGES
AND DISADVANTAGES OF MERGER WITH REGARD
TO EACH BUSINESS FUNCTION

INTEGRATION AND EVALUATION OF MERGER OBJECTIVES

At this stage, a rough picture should emerge of what the new group
will look like some years after the merger. The advantages and
disadvantages of the goals attained and their consequences, the
weighing and comparing of chances of development in each area,
and the possibilities and limitations of the separate companies, will
determine the shape and the limitations of the form the new concern
is to take.

Here we are concerned with the following kinds of problems:

1 The consequences of building up new or existing (weakened)
   brands.
2 The necessity and possibilities of dividing brand organizations.
3 The relative positions of bulk sales and brand sales.
4 The compatibility of sales through wholesalers and sales direct
   to the retail trade.
5 The coordination of the various commercial organizations with
   the production apparatus.
6 The specialization of production units.
7 Investment required from the point of view of commercial
   desirabilities.
8 Research requirements from the point of view of technical and
   commercial plans.
9 Sales and production possibilities for certain research developments under way in one of the partner companies.

The problem is to find a company structure which offers the
chance of realizing as many advantages as possible, coupled with the
acceptance of as few disadvantages as possible; that is, the optimum.

And this does not only apply to the financial, legal or tax structure; it concerns the economic structure of the new enterprise which is to emerge from the amalgamation. It must be emphasized that this cannot be the work solely of outsiders or experts.

The integration and testing of aims up to the emergence of the new economic shape should be a combined project covering a series of well-prepared talks between managers and experts. The result will then provide that 'unity of wisdom' which is a minimum requirement for a fruitful continuation of talks. Once this point has been reached, the date can also be determined at which the merger may financially and legally be considered to have begun. This date is the measuring point for the valuation of the companies and will almost always occur long before the date on which the merger contract is actually signed.

CONCLUDING POINT: PURPOSE, SHAPE AND DATE OF MERGER ARE KNOWN

This is the moment at which—although only roughly and in broad outline—the units which are to be created from the existing companies, and their aims and the connection between them are known and accepted by all parties. It is also the moment at which the date of the merger is decided. As a result, two other important decisions will be taken almost at once. These are the decision to exchange business data and the decision to show annual figures to external advisers.

ACTIVITY 5–6

Minimum period: 2 months
Maximum period: 6 months

STARTING POINT: DECISION TO EXCHANGE BUSINESS DATA

QUANTIFICATION OF ACTION PLANS

The pattern of aims developed under Activity 3–4 requires to be quantified. On production, research and development and sales we must know, not only what can be attained, but also what the consequences will be on costs, yield, share in the market, product ranges, etc., and for the investments required. An investment plan, including stock development, forms the nucleus of this stage. On the basis of turnover forecasts for each group of products (quantities and prices), approximate calculations should be made to determine possible levels of costs and the financial requirements, if the investments are combined and production and buying rationalized.

The completion of this process often means that the plans have to be added to or altered.

CONCLUDING POINT: FORECASTS FOR SEVERAL YEARS
ON THE BASIS OF ACTION PLANS

At this moment we possess—on the basis of action plans drawn up—forecasts for several years of costs, yields and investments.

See Comment 5.

Minimum period: 2 weeks
Maximum period: 3 months

STARTING POINT: PURPOSE, SHAPE AND DATE
OF MERGER ARE KNOWN

ALTERNATIVE FINANCIAL AND CORPORATE STRUCTURE

On the basis of the proposed (economic) structure (5) we can now
investigate what financial-legal structures might be considered.

The aim is to find a number of alternatives. For this we may get in
an expert, or the companies may consider the possibilities themselves, but in that case it will be necessary to consult existing
literature on the possibilities. Some of the problems and concepts
which will have to be discussed are:

1 The choice between a merger of units, a merger of shares, a
merger by means of a partnership.
2 The choice between establishing a new holding company, with
the existing firms as working companies, or the conversion of
one of the existing firms into a holding company.
3 The problem of keeping certain parts of the companies outside
the merger (creation of separate limited companies), division
of companies, etc.
4 Taking account in the business structure of the possibility of a
further extension of the concern by take-overs or subsequent
mergers.

CONCLUDING POINT: COMPLETION OF ALTERNATIVE
FINANCIAL-LEGAL STRUCTURES

A small number of alternative possibilities under company law
have been prepared; all other possibilities have been rejected for
reasons of policy.

ACTIVITY 5–11

Minimum period: 1 month
Maximum period: 6 months

STARTING POINT: DECISION TO SHOW ANNUAL
FIGURES TO INDEPENDENT ADVISERS

INVESTIGATIONS OF PROFITABILITY AND INTRINSIC
VALUE

1 VALUATIONS. The fixed asset and machinery of the companies must be valued by equal standards. Valuations must be uniform, that is to say that, not only should the same criteria be applied but the companies should also be valued by a professional valuer. It must be decided, among other things, who shall carry out the valuation, what shall be valued (fixed assets and machinery, means of transport, possibly also stocks), what the criteria for the valuation will be (going concern value, market value, replacement value, etc.), the valuation date, who shall pay for the valuations and the manner of payment, to whom the valuation reports are to be sent.

Sometimes, valuation reports can be used which have been drawn up for insurance purposes. Sometimes—especially in mergers of very big concerns—a valuation is simply impossible. In these cases, one must work exclusively on the basis of the balance sheets, and estimate hidden reserves.

2 INVESTIGATION OF ASSETS AND EARNING CAPACITY. We must see to what extent the items from the annual figures which have not been valued, must be adapted in order to assess the intrinsic values and the earning-power. Here, too, we must not only have one criterion, but also one man or body to carry out the valuations, to guarantee absolute uniformity.

Determining the intrinsic value means considering the valuation of:

(a) Stocks.
(b) Intangible assets such as patents and licences.

(c) Participations.

(d) Pension rights.

(e) Tax provisions (dormancies, contingencies, unabsorbed losses, and compensatable losses).

(f) Provisions covering the service on products supplied and claims.

(g) Provisions for doubtful debts.

(h) Duration and rate of interest of loans.

Determining the prospective earning power involves:

(a) The depreciation policy adopted by the companies.

(b) Incidental losses.

(c) The valuation of special development possibilities.

(d) Dormant investment charges.

(e) The comparison of salary systems, old age provisions, remuneration of directors, etc.

CONCLUDING POINT: BASIC INFORMATION
FOR VALUATION COMPLETE

ACTIVITY 7–8

Minimum period: 1 week
Maximum period: 1 month

STARTING POINT: ALTERNATIVE FINANCIAL-LEGAL
STRUCTURES COMPLETED

ASPECTS OF TAXATION

Now the taxation consequences of the alternative legal structures must be examined. For shareholders this will include income tax, surtax, capital gains tax and stamp duty. For companies, turnover taxes, taxes on profits and capital gains, stamp duty and registration fees and relief for losses. For family companies, in certain countries, the ability to minimize taxation or profits required for development.

We may find that the financial-legal structure suited to the economic structure has very undesirable consequences with regard to taxation, and vice versa.

This examination is almost impossible without an expert. Ideally, he should, of course, be acceptable to all parties.

CONCLUDING POINT: THE COMPANY STRUCTURES
SUITABLE FOR TAXATION ARE KNOWN

Several structures will now emerge which would be suitable for the new company(ies), that are acceptable as regards taxation— although they will require smaller or greater sacrifices from the taxable parties—and are not objectionable to those concerned.

ACTIVITY 9 (6/8)–10

Minimum period: 1 week
Maximum period: 6 weeks

STARTING POINT: (6) SEVERAL YEARS' FORECAST
ON THE BASIS OF ACTION PLANS
(8) LEGAL STRUCTURES SUITABLE FOR TAXATION

INVESTMENT PRIORITIES VERSUS SOURCES OF FINANCE

The companies which are to be merged each have their own
financial structure. An analysis of these is required. (What, for
instance, is the proportion of outside capital, what are the credit
limits on loans, what is the loan duration, what financing possibilities are there to fall back on, what are the possibilities of extending
the owner's capital? etc.) These analyses put together will give an
insight into the financial shape as it will be after the merger.

The forecasts of yields, costs and investments (6) will enable one
to draw conclusions with regard to, e.g. cash flow, investments,
financing and redemption possibilities through depreciation,
operating results versus the investment plan, etc.

The tax consequences of the future structure are also known (8).
The result of these for the liquidity and the financial structure after
the merger can therefore be examined.

By adding and grouping the data it now becomes possible to
consolidate the annual figures of the merging companies, to forecast
the financial development of the new grouping, and finally to
draw up a financing plan.

CONCLUDING POINT: FORECAST OF CONSOLIDATED
ANNUAL FIGURES FOR SEVERAL YEARS

This forecast, and also the result of the investigation into the
legal structures suitable for taxation may show that the desired
developments laid down in the action plans are not, or not completely, realizable (e.g. because of a lack of financing possibilities).
In that case a feed-back to 5 is necessary to see in what way an
alteration of the action plans might result in a realizable plan.

ACTIVITY 10-13 (a)

Minimum period: 1 month
Maximum period: 3 months

STARTING POINT: FORECAST OF CONSOLIDATED
ANNUAL FIGURES FOR SEVERAL YEARS

ELABORATION OF CORPORATE DEVELOPMENT
PROGRAMME

After the completion of the financing plan, the provisional company
development plan can be finished. This will result in a number of
definite agreements as to:

1 The buying arrangements regarding after the merger.
2 The re-grouping of production capacity.
3 The standardization of products, semi-manufactures and
  designs.
4 The commercial re-grouping, retainment and/or abandoning
  of brands, the entry into new markets.
5 Integration or re-grouping of research and development.
6 Mechanization or automation of administration.
7 Planning and developing of financial structure.

CONCLUDING POINT: MERGER CONTRACT NOW
POSSIBLE WITH A VIEW TO THE PROVISIONAL COMPANY
DEVELOPMENT PLAN

At this moment the economic shape is known, as are the
roads along which the business structure is to be developed, and
the financial consequences of an approach to this development.

ACTIVITY 10-13 (b)

Minimum period: 4 weeks
Maximum period: 6 months

STARTING POINT: FORECAST OF CONSOLIDATED
ANNUAL FIGURES FOR SEVERAL YEARS

DETERMINATION OF FINANCIAL-LEGAL STRUCTURE

Once the financial developments which are to be expected are
known, a definite choice can be made from the legal structures
suitable for taxation. For shareholders, the alternative structures
may have widely differing fiscal consequences, but in company law
the possibilities and consequences are also extremely varied (family
holding, trusts, key directorships, priorities, voting agreements).
This problem is rather intangible and will therefore need repeated
consultations, especially in the case of family firms.

With the help of proposals showing the consequences to private
and business interests, a choice is finally made as to the financial-
legal structure.

CONCLUDING POINT: MERGER CONTRACT CAN BE DRAWN
UP WITH A VIEW TO FINANCIAL-LEGAL STRUCTURE

See Comment 6.

ACTIVITY II–I3

Minimum period: 1 month
Maximum period: 6 months

STARTING POINT: BASIC INFORMATION FOR VALUATION COMPLETED

The moment arrives when the valuations of fixed and current assets has been completed, the taxation consequences are known and the reserves and provisions have been determined. This is also the moment at which the work can be started on determining from the data the value of each of the participating companies.

DETERMINATION OF THE EXCHANGE RATIO

With the help of the information which has been gathered, one can now draw up for each of the merging companies:

1 A balance sheet which will show as clearly as possible the intrinsic value of the company and its components.
2 A profit and loss account showing, as clearly as possible, the prospective earning capacity.

These two items form the main, and sometimes even the only foundation for advice on the exchange ratio.

To be able to relate the two factors, profitability must be expressed as a value. The connection between the two values—the valuation formula—may vary greatly. Here there are no standard guides. The formula applied—the relation between intrinsic and profitability value, valuation of surplus profits or capitalization of profit—depends on the complex aims underlying the merger.

For instance, if the idea is to join forces in order to forge ahead commercially, then the intrinsic value will be dominant. If the point is to consolidate and stabilize profits, the profitability value is the more important the longer it may be expected to last.

There may be a third factor in the valuation formula—the yield on the shares—if the companies concerned are quoted on the Stock Exchange. The dividend policy and the Stock Exchange prices are

by no means negligible, and, in some cases are even dominant
factors in determining the proportionate value.

Apart from the proportionate value of the companies, there are
other factors which also influence the advisable share exchange
ratio:

1 The extent to which a financial settlement between the parties
   (either in shares and/or in money) is possible and desirable.
2 The wish, in order to provide against undesirable changes in
   company or management, to give the smallest party a certain
   minimum block of shares.
3 Special considerations, such as the positive or negative value of
   exceptional liquidity, the sacrifice of special opportunities for
   the sake of the larger future concern, etc.

CONCLUDING POINT: MERGER CONTRACT CAN BE DRAWN
    UP WITH A VIEW TO DECIDING ON CASH OR SHARE
                         EXCHANGE

ACTIVITY 12 (6/7)–13

Minimum period: 2 weeks
Maximum period: 2 months

STARTING POINT: (6) FORECAST FOR SEVERAL YEARS
ON THE BASIS OF ACTION PLANS. (7) ALTERNATIVE
FINANCIAL-LEGAL STRUCTURES COMPLETED

STRUCTURING TOP AND SUBSIDIARY MANAGEMENT

Existing regulations and position will disappear. New tasks will be
laid down for those executives whose positions will essentially
change because of the merger. We shall have to find the answer to
questions such as:

1 Who is to be on the board?
2 What positions should be created with regard to concern
  management and working company levels?
3 Who are to fill these positions?
4 What will be the responsibilities, power, activities, rewards and
  pensions for these positions?
5 What will be the connection between the position at the top
  and the activities to be carried out?
6 What will be the relation between managerial powers in the
  holding company and those in the working company?

It is best if a retirement and succession plan is drawn up as a
basis for binding agreements on these points.

CONCLUDING POINT: MERGER CONTRACT CAN BE
DRAWN UP FOR TOP MANAGEMENT STRUCTURE

A complete proposal is now available in which all the organizational consequences for top management structure have been taken
into account.
See Comment 7.

Minimum period: 1 month
Maximum period: 3 months

STARTING POINT: MERGER CONTRACT CAN NOW BE
DRAFTED

Advice on the cash/share exchange is available.
The financial-legal structure is known.
The provisional company development plan is completed.
The proposal for top management is known.

In other words, at this moment the basic data for the structure
of the merger is available. All the component parts for the new
group are here. They must now be welded together to form a whole.

DRAFTING THE MERGER AGREEMENT

The group of people concerned in realizing the merger consists of
several parties, each with its own interests, and therefore each with
a very different appreciation of the various aspects presented by
the merger.

For example, some will consider the cash/share exchange the heart
of the matter, and will pay special attention to settling this point
in the contract. This will include the conditions under which the
offer is to be made, and conditions regarding a cancellation of the
transaction. Others will set special store by the position their top
executives will have in the management structure of the new
company. Some may also consider the development plan of primary
importance; this plan cannot be allowed to fail and they wish to
settle the chief agreements of this plan firmly, and possibly, even
to have them included in the contract. Others again will above all
stress the financial-legal structure and possibly the private financial
consequences of it.

It is, therefore, advisable to make an inventory, first in each
company and then in the group of people representing the parties
concerned, of all the points which must be included in the merger
contract. One can then obtain an exhaustive list or a provisional

agreement, which can then be further drafted into a satisfactory contract by a solicitor.

CONCLUDING POINT: DRAFT OF MERGER CONTRACT COMPLETED

We now have a document (or a number of documents) which can serve as a basis for the final negotiations.

ACTIVITY 14–15

Minimum period: 1 month
Maximum period: 3 months

STARTING POINT: DRAFT OF MERGER CONTRACT
COMPLETED

NEGOTIATIONS

The ideas, opinions and documents submitted to the solicitor have now been set out in legal terms in the merger contract. This precise wording forces everyone to realize exactly what is going to happen. Obscurities, misrepresentations and errors will require correction or negotiation. The structure of the merger will be altered and amended and these changes will be added to the contract. With the help of these documents the last differences of opinion should now be cleared away. The contract will then be adapted to include the final agreements.

CONCLUDING POINT: SIGNING OF MERGER CONTRACT

The corrected merger contract is signed. The merger has become a fact and can now be announced as such to the employees of the company and to the public, provided there is no question of approval by the authorities.

ACTIVITY 14–20

Minimum period: 1 day
Maximum period: 1 week

STARTING POINT: DRAFT OF MERGER CONTRACT
COMPLETED

PREPARATION OF THE MERGER ANNOUNCEMENT

The announcement must be prepared, for once the contract has been signed an announcement becomes urgent. It can happen that companies are obliged to announce the merger even before the definite contract has been signed. As far as the announcement is concerned, one must distinguish between the external and the internal publication. The internal announcement poses problems of distinguishing between categories of employees (top executives, other employees, works committee, trade unions), deciding in which order these groups will be informed and what the exact contents of the statement will be to each group. The timing of the announcement to the various groups is also of importance.

For the external publication, the moment of announcement is of primary importance (this is especially true for companies quoted on the Stock Exchange). An announcement will have to be made to the Press. Its contents must be decided and a decision made as to which (if any) people should be notified in advance (with the obligation of embargo).

The question will arise of whether a Press Conference should be held and if so, who is to be present and who will speak.

CONCLUDING POINT: THE MERGER CONTRACT HAS
BEEN SIGNED; THE MERGER HAS BEEN ANNOUNCED
BOTH INTERNALLY AND TO THE PUBLIC

UNIFICATION OF MANAGEMENT: PHASE 20-x-y

After the financial-legal unification has become a fact, there is a period during which management must be unified, so that the moment may come when actual growth may begin, or—in other words—when the concern really exists as an entity in its own right and is not simply an amalgamation of two groups.

See Comment 8.

Minimum period: 1 week
Maximum period: 1 month

STARTING POINT: THE SIGNING OF THE CONTRACT
AND THE ANNOUNCEMENT OF THE MERGER

INSTALLATION OF TOP MANAGEMENT

One of the first things to be done immediately after the merger contract has been signed, is to see that the new top management structure becomes operative. This does not yet apply to the management of the working companies, for they will, for the moment, continue as they are and will carry on as much as possible with the existing management. What must be settled now is the master-management at the top (see pages 142–150). This management must be officially appointed, and concrete arrangements must be made so that executive management can freely carry out its work.

If the executives concerned are already on the management of the working companies, they will have to be freed sufficiently to carry out their new tasks, and the vacancies thus created must be adequately filled, so that during the difficult transitional period the working companies have a strong leadership. Transition from tasks prior to the merger to tasks after the merger must be settled.

The aim is to build up the management structure in such a way as to guarantee the success of the merger.

CONCLUDING POINT: MANAGEMENT INSTALLED

Tasks, powers, responsibilities, office space, etc., of the new group's management and managements of the working companies have now been settled and put into effect.

ACTIVITY 21-22

Minimum period: 1 month
Maximum period: 6 months

STARTING POINT: MANAGEMENT INSTALLED

MARKETING AND PRODUCT ANALYSES

Although the company development plan (13) gave a rough picture
of the structure which, in due course, would result from the merged
firms, the investigations are never extended beyond the point
required at that stage. Up to that moment it is always possible that
the merger will fail, and it should again be noted that the exchange
of data is sometimes restricted.

To complete the company development plan, a market investigation and product analysis are almost always essential. All the data
from the partner companies which has not yet been revealed must
now be taken into account, so that products, their ranges, quantitative and qualitative production capacities, market positions, etc.,
can be fully compared.

Once this complete survey is available, a detailed examination of
the outside position can be made. This may mean that activities
must be extended beyond a market investigation or product
analysis. Other investigations may be required, such as an examination of the structure of the branch of industry, of export possibilities,
packing, product development, manufacture, etc. The aim is to
obtain knowledge of markets, products, production capacities, etc.,
and to get a clear insight into the relative position of the group.

The investigations will have to be listed, committees will have to
be appointed, perhaps including outsiders, and tasks will have to
be allotted; periods within which certain results are expected must
be fixed. In this phase there is again a vital use of the system of
network planning.

CONCLUDING POINT: DETAILED INVESTIGATIONS
COMPLETED

The result is a detailed knowledge of the foundations of the
action plans and of the relative position of the concern.

ACTIVITY 21-23

Minimum period: 2 months
Maximum period: 6 months

STARTING POINT: MANAGEMENT INSTALLED

HARMONIZATION OF ACCOUNTS AND FINANCIAL
ADMINISTRATION

The first step towards central management is to unify and centralize
financial control, and the initial phase in this is to unify the accounting systems and financial control. A committee, consisting of an
independent accountant (or any auditor) and one or more of the
directors generally carries out this process and introduces the
system, for a uniform accounts system and the uniform *application*
of such a system are two very different things.

We must also decide how many accounts there will be and how
the financial control can be centralized as quickly as possible. Will
the existing customs of payment and authority to act be maintained
for a while, or must these be unified and centralized as soon as
possible?

Such decisions may have a drastic effect on working patterns
and cause reactions in the various companies, although central
control of the flow of money must obviously be effected more
rapidly.

CONCLUDING POINT: ACCOUNTING SYSTEM AND
FINANCIAL ADMINISTRATION REALIZED

See Comment 9.

ACTIVITY 21-26

Minimum period: 1 month
Maximum period: 4 months

STARTING POINT: NEW MANAGEMENT INSTALLED

ESTABLISHING CENTRAL PRODUCTION PLANNING

In many cases it is important to have the central planning for the
co-ordination of the working companies available at an early
stage. Furthermore, it is practically impossible to develop the
group into its final shape without having a central body which is
constantly in complete charge of the relationship between the
different production units and also between production and commercial departments.

Central planning and progress control are part of a central
control system which ensures that all parts of the new company
stay on the right track during the intricate process of alteration.
The realization of a central planning department demands, in
the first place, an extensive analysis of the existing systems in the
various companies. A uniform system must be developed and
introduced.

Part of the actual unification of the planning in the various
companies may also have to wait until the production departments
have been joined up. In any case, this problem of planning must
be tackled at an early stage, in order to get a clear idea of the
existing systems and of the way in which an efficient central system
can be achieved.

CONCLUDING POINT: PLANS FOR CENTRAL PLANNING
COMPLETED

The planning has been unified and is commanded centrally.
See Comment 10.

ACTIVITY 21–28(a)

Minimum period: 1 month
Maximum period: 4 months

STARTING POINT: NEW MANAGEMENT INSTALLED

COMMERCIAL HARMONIZATION

Immediately after the merger has been effected and announced, a dangerous situation arises commercially. Competitors have been alarmed by the merger and will try to benefit as much as possible from any internal confusion. They may even make extra efforts to bring this about.

Moreover, there is sometimes a tendency for the merged companies to adopt a wait-and-see attitude, affording new opportunities to their competitors.

What is needed now is:

1 Immediate categorization of customers, ways of approach, credit conditions, and other selling conditions, prices, special cases of competition, overlapping groups of products, etc.
2 A plan which—in general terms—accentuates the useful differences between the partners and eliminates obviously unprofitable ones. This means arrangements regarding internal competition, agreements concerning prices, conditions and calls, a *limited* exchange of customers suppliers, product range agreements, etc.
3 Internal 'briefing' of all those concerned with sales both 'inside' and 'outside'. Each of these people must know where competition will be continued in the same way, where it will change, where it will be lifted and what outsiders should be told if conversation turns to the merger.
4 An extra keen commercial campaign with representatives, advertising, etc., so that by means of a vigorous continuation of the 'old' profitable competition—against a harmonious background—third parties are prevented from benefiting from the merger.

By maintaining sales, at the same time eliminating evidently ineffective competition, the commercial framework is provided for the integration which is to come (much) later.

CONCLUDING POINT: THE CONCERN IS VIABLE:
REGULATIONS HAVE BEEN HARMONIZED AND CUSTOMS
COMPLETED

ACTIVITY 21–28 (b)

Minimum period: 1 month
Maximum period: 4 months

STARTING POINT: NEW MANAGEMENT INSTALLED

HARMONIZING PERSONNEL POLICY

An important 'short-term aspect', which must be tackled as soon as possible after the signing of the contract, is a listing of all regulations and customs relating to personnel in the combined companies, so that either a system of gradual convergence, or an immediate harmonization can be effected. Apart from the fact that once the merger has been announced, employees from the various companies will begin to exchange data, the moment will come when employees will have to work side by side. If, at that time, there are still considerable differences in regulations and usages, problems are inevitable.

It is, therefore, very important to co-ordinate the regulations applying to personnel such as remunerations and salaries, collective agreements, old age provisions, secondary employment conditions, 'perks' (cars, houses belonging to the company), bonuses and shares in the profit, extra provisions (e.g insurance facilities), works committees, working hours, savings schemes, staff clubs, etc. The aim in each case is to prevent the personnel from marking time and so hampering the progress of the merger. An extensive inventory of existing regulations and usages will always be necessary in order to evolve a uniform regulation which—if not a sum of the existing regulations—will, at any rate, guarantee that there will in future be equal treatment of all employees.

CONCLUDING POINT: CONCERN VIABLE: REGULATIONS
HARMONIZED AND USAGES COMPLETED

The chief differences in personnel regulations and custom have been eliminated. For the remainder a system of gradual approximation has been set under way.

ACTIVITY 22-25

Minimum period: 6 weeks
Maximum period: 4 months

STARTING POINT: DETAILED INVESTIGATIONS COMPLETED

SPECIFICATION OF CORPORATE DEVELOPMENT AND
INVESTMENT PROGRAMME

The detailed investigations now enable us to elaborate the development plan drawn up during the period before the merger into a
series of coherent and detailed action plans for every field.

Detailed programmes are drawn up for:

1 The commercial development of a new policy for brand
  articles.
2 The approaching of certain export markets.
3 The parallel approach to wholesale and retail organizations.
4 Modernizing production methods.
5 Improving production plant by scrapping obsolete machines,
  by a better disposition of equipment, possibly by buying new
  machines.
6 A re-distribution of production and administration over the
  available buildings, possibly planning a new building.
7 Developing new products or packaging.
8 The transfer, retraining and job rotation of personnel.

The results of these action plans will enable forecasts to be made
in different fields, e.g. turnover per product group, production
capacities, investments, liquidity, etc. An investment plan showing
the amount and time of expenditures for production, sales, product
development and administration during the next few years can
also be drawn up.

For this rather complex pattern, a survey must be made showing
these developments as a coherent group of activities. A new network
will therefore emerge illustrating all the changes which will take
place after the concern has become changeable.

A number of new networks may emerge for different periods—
for instance, the first six-month period generally requires greater

exactitude than the survey covering the next five years. The aim is to create an integrated working plan covering several years, with obligatory periodic reports from the working companies down to the lowest level, and set down both in terms of management and in terms of finance.

CONCLUDING POINT: FOUNDATIONS OF FINANCIAL CONTROL (WORKING PLAN, CONCERN DEVELOPMENT AND INVESTMENT PLAN COVERING SEVERAL YEARS) COMPLETED

The network for the development of the concern, the investment plan based on this network and the elaborate financial planning have now been completed.

ACTIVITY 23-24

Minimum period: 2 months
Maximum period: 9 months

STARTING POINT: ONE ACCOUNTS SYSTEM; ONE SYSTEM
OF FINANCIAL ADMINISTRATION

UNIFICATION OF WRITTEN COMMUNICATIONS AND
REPORTS

The existing business reports must be adapted and developed into
a central system of reports and sources of information. This is part
of the activities which lead to central control.

Some of the points which will have to be dealt with are:

1 Determining the measuring-points for production and sales
  data in the various parts of the business. This includes surveys
  of production, of turnover, of orders including contract price
  versus costs of personnel including internal and external changes,
  and of stock.

2 Determining the exact contents of the surveys and the fre-
  quency and timing at which they must be produced.

3 The use which is to be made of the data (who will judge them
  and how?).

This stage consists of categorizing the present situation, planning
an adapted system and introducing it.

CONCLUDING POINT: CENTRAL SYSTEM OF REPORTS
AND SOURCES OF INFORMATION

A uniform system of reports is now available. Data is gathered
at a central point and it is possible to issue information of any
deviations centrally.

ACTIVITY 23–25

Minimum period: 2 months
Maximum period: 9 months

STARTING POINT: SINGLE SYSTEMS FOR ACCOUNTS
AND FINANCIAL ADMINISTRATION

INTEGRATION OF BOOK-KEEPING AND COSTING
DEPARTMENTS

Once the accounting systems are unified, the book-keeping can also
be integrated.

1 The need will arise immediately for further numerical coherence
in such items as the coding of stock, debtors and orders.
Attention must also be paid to the grouping and analyses of
figures, unified wage systems and similar matters.

2 The next step must be the analysis of the flow of forms and
the administrative actions required to arrive at standard
forms and cards, etc.

N.B. It is at this point that any extreme aspirations towards
mechanization and centralization must be firmly checked.

3 After this—whilst retaining the existing geographical decentra-
lization of personnel—uniform calculation methods, systems
of wage calculation, stock control methods can be tried out
(preferably not using new systems, but trying an existing one).
   At this stage it must be clear who will be the future leaders,
group managers, etc., in the administration and what are the
objectives set for executive personnel.

4 As these tests proceed, consideration should be given to
whether certain sections—book-keeping, invoicing, stock control, salaries, wages, and so on—should now be centralized
in view of the progress of the merger.

5 The furthest one can go at this stage—and often one cannot
go so far—is the geographical linking of centralized sections.

CONCLUDING POINT: FOUNDATIONS OF FINANCIAL
CONTROL COMPLETED

Accounting has now been integrated; the book-keeping departments have been centralized as much as possible or even integrated. Book-keeping, invoicing, and the administration of wages and salaries is uniform and has been adapted to the aims of the concern.

ACTIVITY 25–27

Minimum period: 2 months
Maximum period: 4 months

STARTING POINT: FOUNDATIONS OF FINANCIAL CONTROL:
LONG-TERM WORKING PLAN FOR GROUP DEVELOPMENT
AND INVESTMENT PLAN: ONE BOOK-KEEPING SYSTEM;
ONE CENTRAL ACCOUNTING SYSTEM: (24) ONE CENTRAL
REPORTING AND INFORMATION SYSTEM

ESTABLISHMENT OF PROFITABILITY AND LIQUIDITY
CONTROL

A system is required which will not only enable the management to
judge the earning power and liquidity of the concern periodically
(preferably as soon as possible after the end of each period), but
which will also make it possible to analyse speedily the causes of
different developments.

At this stage in the integration of the management structure the
following are available: the company development plan, the
investment plan and liquidity estimate, the data concerning
integrated book-keeping and adequate business statistics. Long-term
control of the development plan will consist of periodic comparisons
of forecasts and actual results, investigation of the consequences of
any differences, and measures to correct these differences or adapt
the plans. In the same way, a central department for short-term
planning will exercise control over the mutual adaptation of
production departments, or of production and commerce.

For long-term control we shall periodically need interim profit
and loss statements showing the results for each period and the
cumulative results, on the basis of, and compared with, the annual
budget.

The difficulty here is mostly movement of goods: points at which
this movement can best be measured must be considered.

CONCLUDING POINT: CENTRAL ORIENTATION: CENTRAL LIQUIDITY AND EARNING POWER REPORTS

Frequent and up-to-date reports are now available which give a clear picture of the earning power and liquidity of the concern, and are comparable with our forecasts.

ACTIVITY 26–27

Minimum period: 2 months
Maximum period: 6 months

STARTING POINT: FRAMEWORK OF CENTRAL PLANNING COMPLETED; (24) ONE CENTRAL SYSTEM FOR REPORTS AND INFORMATION

ESTABLISHMENT OF PROGRESS CONTROL

The central reports and information system must be developed so that there is enough data available in the production departments in order to enable the management to exercise progress control on planning and complete the central planning by a system of production control.

This activity primarily includes decisions on what is required for progress control of planning, the way in which this data will be supplied to the planners, and the way in which data will subsequently be used in a central planning department.

CONCLUDING POINT: CENTRAL PLANNING

We now have a central planning department enabling the management to exercise full production control.

ACTIVITY 27–28

Minimum period: 2 months
Maximum period: 9 months

STARTING POINT: CENTRAL PLANNING

ESTABLISHMENT OF OPERATIONAL CONTROL

As soon as central earning power and liquidity reports are coming in, production control in the various companies has been realized and the required coherence between the various reports has been attained by the central planning department, then real management control will become possible.

This control may take different shapes. It may be the task of one member of the management. The problem is to find a man who has both the management abilities and the time for the task.

Another solution is to direct the different data to one executive—a comptroller—who will undertake the time-consuming interpretation work, prepare decisions for the management and, via the lower management, be able to develop the required central managerial control. Sometimes it may also be necessary to establish a central executive department to recapitulate and interpret this data.

Whether one opts for a comptroller or for a department, it is essential to have a plan which will not only make it possible to interpret the data which is now freely available, but which also has the power to suggest or introduce corrective measures, or to take measures which will lead to change in the existing plans.

Here, therefore, insight is required into the growth and development of the concern and the purposes of the merger, for without it, interpretation of the data, let alone any real managerial control, will be impossible.

A well-planned and detailed company development plan will sufficiently indicate those aspects of data which are of paramount importance for the development of the concern. Once alterations have begun, the department or the executive will also have the task of drawing up new or adapted forecasts in various fields. In this sense, changes are not only forecast but also controlled.

CONCLUDING POINT: CONTROL OF THE COMBINED
COMPANIES IS NOW COMPLETE

Development can now be followed and acted upon as soon as there are any deviations from the plan.

See Comment 11.

ACTIVITY 28–X

RE-ORGANIZATION OF THE BUSINESS

STARTING POINT: CONTROL COMPLETE

As soon as we have a long-term detailed development plan (22–25), a central business-economic control system (25/26–27–28), and the necessary harmonizing measures in sales and personnel management have been realized (21–28), the moment has come to start realizing the development plan. The process of change will have different consequences, different critical stages and moments, according to the nature of the aims envisaged with the merger, the kind of merger and the extent of the changes.

On an average, these changes might consist of the following stages (which should begin more or less simultaneously):

1 Centralized purchasing.
2 Specialization and standardization of product designs, products, semi-manufactures, and raw materials.
3 Production specialization.
4 Commercial re-organization.
5 Integration of research and development.
6 Administrative re-organization.
7 Take-over of companies.

ACTIVITY 20–30

Minimum period: 1 month
Maximum period: 2 months

STARTING POINT: MERGER CONTRACT HAS BEEN
SIGNED, AND MERGER ANNOUNCED

FULFILMENT OF LEGAL OBLIGATIONS

The formalities required and conditions of the merger contract
must be realized. This is one of the activities which must be set
in motion as soon as the contract has been signed, for as long as the
conditions of the contract have not been fulfilled, or only partially,
there can be no question of a completed agreement and there is
always a risk of disagreement, revocation or of an alteration in the
conditions.

Points to be remembered here are:

1 Adoption of resolutions at shareholders' meetings.
2 Drawing up the Articles of Memorandum and Association
   of the holding company and obtaining any legal opinions
   required.
3 In certain countries, submitting requests concerning taxation
   consequences, to the appropriate revenue authorities.
4 Registration, under the Companies Act, of the holding company.
5 Placing and exchange of shares and the formalizing of additional capital introduced.
6 The realization of changes in the Articles of Association of
   existing companies, etc.

Here again contractual conditions will vary from one merger to
another and the required activities will therefore also vary.

CONCLUDING POINT: STATUTORY AND LEGAL
CONDITIONS OF THE CONTRACT HAVE BEEN FULFILLED

ACTIVITY 30–31 (a)

Minimum period: 1 month
Maximum period: 5 months

STARTING POINT: LEGAL AND STATUTORY CONDITIONS
OF CONTRACT HAVE BEEN FULFILLED

RATIONALIZING OF FINANCIAL RESOURCES

Credit rationalization includes negotiations with banks, institutional investors and other financiers, which are aimed at simplifying the financial structure, providing the extra finances required for the plans which are to be realized, and at financing the concern in the most advantageous way.

Credit rationalization may include:

1 Concentrating credits on a limited number of banks.
2 Unifying loan conditions (type of interest, duration, redemption obligations, security requirements, borrowing limits, etc.).
3 Obtaining better terms of credit.
4 Share transactions.

CONCLUDING POINT: FINANCIAL STRUCTURE READY
FOR ADAPTATION

Once negotiations and investigations regarding the financial structure have been completed and a Consolidated Balance Sheet is prepared, the financial structure can be rationalized.

ACTIVITY 30–31 (b)

Minimum period: 1 month
Maximum period: 3 months

STARTING POINT: LEGAL AND STATUTORY CONDITIONS
OF CONTRACT HAVE BEEN FULFILLED

CONSOLIDATION OF BALANCES BY EXTERNAL ACCOUNTANT

Consolidated balance sheets are an essential requirement for credit
rationalization. At this stage in the merger, it is not yet possible to
obtain these from the company's own accounts department. An
accountant must produce a consolidated annual document from
the books available.

CONCLUDING POINT: ONCE THE INVESTIGATIONS AND
TALKS CONCERNING CREDIT RATIONALIZATION HAVE
BEEN COMPLETED AND A CONSOLIDATED BALANCE
SHEET PRODUCED, THE FINANCIAL STRUCTURE OF THE
CONCERN CAN BE EFFECTED

ACTIVITY 31–y

STARTING POINT: FINANCIAL STRUCTURE READY FOR
ADAPTATION

FINANCIAL RE-ORGANIZATION

A number of activities can now be undertaken, such as the concentration of credits in one bank, the transfer of credits from banks to institutional investors, or vice versa, alterations in financial agreements, the arrangement of securities for superannuation funds, the revision or transfer of mortgage agreements, issues of shares, debentures, etc.

TIME-PLANNING WITH THE HELP OF THE PLAN

In practice it is helpful to make use of a network in dealing with Activity 2–3; that is: 'getting to grips with the merger.' Needless to say, each case may demand a different sequence of activities or even, in part, different activities altogether.

Special attention must be given to individual situations and it is useful to see what time margin there is to deal with incidental issues. This shows exactly how long these can be delayed for the sake of the critical activities which determine the duration of the merger process. The best way of approaching this time-planning is by discussing the matter, estimating the time (or possibly the maximum and minimum time) required for each activity, and then making a short calculation in the form of tables. There is an example of such tables, *on the basis of the minimum periods* experienced in simple cases, when such activities have been fully completed according to the plan. The tables include the stages 1–20 (Table 1) and 20–28 (Table 2) of the plan (Numbers 30 and 31 are irrelevant to time planning).

The tables have been drawn up as follows: Firstly the activities have been systematically arranged in a column according to their starting and concluding points (Columns 1 and 2) (in numbering points in the plan, care has been taken that no activity is ever preceded in sequence by one with a lower number). The estimated duration in weeks then follows in Column 3. Then the maximum number of weeks have been calculated for each activity which separate it from the beginning and end of the stage concerned (Columns 4 and 5). Because of the systematic arrangement of Columns 1, 2 and 3 it is easy to make this calculation from the table (without making use of the plan). By adding up Columns 4 and 5 we have the number of weeks which the entire stage will take, in so far as this depends on the activity concerned (Column 6). The maximum number of weeks found in Column 6 is therefore the total duration of the stage.

The difference between the stage duration and the numbers found in Column 6 indicates the number of weeks by which the activity concerned can be delayed with impunity—the 'latitude' (Column 7). All the cases where latitude=zero are critical and determine the

Table 1: Point 1 to Point 20—Note that the estimated duration of each activity was given in months. In this table 1 month=4 weeks. Activities estimated in days are given here as 1 week.

1	2	3	4	5	6	7
Activity		Minimum duration of activity in weeks	Duration from the beginning of the operation to Point 20 in weeks	Duration from Point 1 to the beginning of the operation in weeks	Total of Columns 4 and 5	Latitude: Column 6–34 weeks (0=Critical Path)
Beginning	End					
1– 2		4	34	0	34	0
2– 3		1	30	4	34	0
3– 4		4	29	5	34	0
3– 4		4	29	5	34	0
3– 4		4	29	5	34	0
4– 5		4	25	9	34	0
5– 6		8	21	13	34	0
5– 6		8	21	13	34	0
5– 6		8	21	13	34	0
5– 7		2	16	13	29	5
5–11		4	16	13	29	5
5–11		4	16	13	29	5
6– 9		0	13	21	34	0
6–12		0	10	21	31	3
7– 8		1	14	15	29	5
7–12		0	10	15	25	9
8– 9		0	13	16	29	5
8–11		0	12	16	28	6
9–10		1	13	21	34	0
10–13		4	12	22	34	2
10–13		4	12	22	34	0
11–13		4	12	17	29	5
12–13		2	10	21	31	3
13–14		4	8	26	34	0
14–15		4	4	30	34	0
14–20		1	1	30	32	2
15–20		0	0	34	34	0

Table 2: Point 20 to Point 28

I	2	3	4	5	6	7
Activity		Minimum duration of activity in weeks	Duration from the beginning of the operation to Point 28 in weeks	Duration from Point 20 to the beginning of the operation in weeks	Total of Columns 4 and 5	Latitude: Column 6–33 weeks (o=Critical Path)
Beginning	End					
20–21		1	33	0	33	0
21–22		4	25	1	26	7
22–23		4	25	1	26	7
22–23		8	32	1	33	0
22–26		4	20	1	21	12
22–28		4	4	1	5	28
22–28		4	4	1	5	28
22–25		6	22	5	27	6
23–24		8	24	9	33	0
23–25		8	24	9	33	0
24–25		0	16	17	33	0
24–26		0	16	17	33	0
25–27		8	16	17	33	0
26–27		8	16	17	33	0
27–28		8	8	25	33	0

duration of the stage. These must therefore be speeded up as much as possible.

The tables show that the critical path in our plan runs as follows: 1–2–3–4–5–6–9–10–13–14–15–20–21–23–24–25/26–27–28. The total duration is $34+33=67$ weeks. We also found that the non-critical activities may be delayed from 3 to 38 weeks. If the critical activities are greatly accelerated, those with little latitude may, in their turn, become critical. If there are any great differences during the merger process, it may therefore be advisable, from time to time, to repeat the calculations on the basis of the most recent data.

All this provides only a rough indication of the use which can be made of network planning in a merger. During the second phase of the merger the matter may become so complicated that the methodical development of the network planning must be considerably refined.

COMMENTS

The network type of working plan described produces all kinds of comments, for opinions may always differ as to what each activity actually is, the actual importance of the order in which the activities should be carried out and the connection between them. The time required for any activity is also open to discussion.

There is no point in giving an exhaustive list of all the comments which could be made, but it is advisable to set down a number of general symptoms and striking developments. These comments are set out separately to keep the working plan and its description as clear as possible and not to clutter it up with the opinions, considerations, warnings, etc.

COMMENT I, FINANCIAL-LEGAL UNIFICATION

If the merger process is not completely clear, this will cause uncertainty or even fear in those concerned. Such feelings are mainly caused by doubts as to their own capacity or career, fear of an unexpected move by one of the negotiating partners, or that one of these partners will take advantage of confidential data, etc. If talks are prolonged, these feelings will increase and may cause irrational reactions of reticence, excessive demands, attempts to negotiate unnegotiable matters, tendencies to give pre-eminence to personal factors, etc. This may often give rise to the very points, for fear of which a partner had originally become suspicious.

It is, therefore, of the utmost importance to structure and plan the merger process, e.g. by means of a network.

The structure will provide a considered sequence and synchronization for the actions and activities which must be carried out. This considered nature of sequence and synchronization will have a salutory psychological effect: everyone knows where he stands. Furthermore, only those steps will be undertaken which, in the process, can be achieved. In other words, no step will be taken until all the data required for that step can be provided as the result of a number of parallel activities.

The planning which is made possible by the network, offers a clear prospect of those critical moments at which a clearly defined part of the work has been completed. The merging companies can work towards definite points. The result is that they can 'relax', and will need less time and attention for emotional problems.

It is clear, therefore, that the structuring and planning of the merger process makes a very substantial contribution to its success.

COMMENT 2, ACTIVITY 1–2. PREPARATORY TALKS

The preparatory talks may take a long time and it is certain that a fairly high percentage of these consultations are unsuccessful. Although a time limit of one–eighteen months is given, there are cases where such preparatory talks have taken over three years.

An important cause of the failure of such talks is often the lack of understanding of the merger process and of the method of approaching a merger. Cases where accountants have been asked to make valuations while there was still no clear understanding as to the purposes aimed at in the merger, are by no means exceptional. Sometimes, even in the mergers of big companies, the matter of the structure-at-the-top of the future concern is discussed when nothing is yet known about the way in which the concern is to operate.

COMMENT 3, ACTIVITY 2–3. DECIDING ON THE MERGER APPROACH

Here again, the worse the understanding of the merger process, the more time the activity will take. For instance: it may not have been recognized that the preliminary talks cannot be combined with determining the way in which the merger must be tackled.

The work involved in this activity varies from one case to another. In general, the more chance there is of the structure of the original companies being drastically affected by the merger, the more complicated (and therefore the more time-demanding) it will be to determine the merger process.

In these early phases of the merger, it is of great importance that the participants should concentrate on the actual business problems rather than on the legal, financial or managerial problems. In practice, partners in these talks often find this extremely difficult.

COMMENT 4, ACTIVITY 3–4. INVESTIGATING THE PURPOSES OF THE MERGER

Occasionally, the purposes aimed at in a merger are clear from the start. Usually, however, the ideas of the partners are limited to a number of generally accepted truths mentioned in every theory on the subject as the advantages of a 'concentration of enterprises'. They do not realize that an entirely new edifice is under construction which will, eventually, in no way resemble any of the merging companies. It will be a company with its own new structure, a new appearance, its own management—in short, an entity which will have to obey the laws which govern bigger companies, if they are to survive, and which differ considerably from the conditions governing smaller companies.

It is, therefore, highly dangerous if the aims of the merger are clear only in appearance. This means not only that the merger process will be fraught with difficulties and delaying factors, the causes of which will not be clear or can no longer be analysed; but also that the realization of the advantages is delayed, and there is even a chance that later—when the aims have at last been examined in detail—there comes the awful realization that it would have been better not to merge in the first place.

The appearance is strongest when high-sounding slogans on the rewards of concentration are too easily adopted instead of studying exactly what the down-to-earth advantages of merging would be, particularly of merging with the particular businesses concerned.

In this respect, however, nature generally has a salutory effect— merger talks die an early death if the point of merging has not been sufficiently investigated and talks are founded on specious arguments without any analytical basis.

Very broadly speaking, the stage of investigating the aims of the merger can only be skipped or restricted to a minimum if it is clear that the economic structure of the merging companies will not be greatly affected, if at all, by the merger. This, however, happens very rarely.

COMMENT 5, ACTIVITY 5–6. QUANTIFICATION OF ACTION PLANS

The duration of this phase naturally depends on how far the plan demands the most intensive investigation. The time required may differ greatly from one merger to another.

The depth required in the investigation depends largely on the type of merger. Obviously, a horizontal, scale-enlarging merger will demand a fairly extensive investigation both in the production sector (production integration) and in the commercial sector (avoidance of turnover loss). In a merger aimed chiefly at increasing the product range, the commercial sector will demand a much more profound investigation than the production sector. In the case of vertical integration, product development combined with production methods may require the most attention. Another important aspect here is the type of business of the merger partners. For instance, the matters which interest a manufacturer of consumer brand articles will generally not be the same as those on which a manufacturer of capital goods must concentrate.

COMMENT 6, ACTIVITY 10–13(b). DETERMINATION OF FINANCIAL AND CORPORATE STRUCTURE

In private companies, the choice of the financial-legal structure is the result of negotiations. Shareholders or members of the family are often closely concerned, and private interests play a major part.

Examples of major factors are:

1 Obtaining marketable stock.
2 Terminating influential shareholder positions.
3 Securing capital by means of strong management (e.g. when there is a risk of weak succession), etc.

In public companies, the management must make the fairest possible choice from the existing alternatives. Whatever their choice, in the shareholders' meeting held to discuss exchange proposal someone is certainly bound to criticize it.

COMMENT 7, ACTIVITY 12–13. STRUCTURING TOP SUBSIDIARY MANAGEMENT

As mentioned before, discussions about the future management structure nearly always start too early. However, many people will disagree about the moment at which these talks should begin. Some people consider, and they are probably right, that the job of welding the merging companies into a new entity will have to be carried out by the new management. Admittedly, if the structure of this management is not successful, it would be better not to merge and thus avoid the risk of failure or of a reconstruction which would drag on for years and cost a considerable amount of money.

The structure of the management, however, is a function of the merger. For that reason, the top organization can only be determined effectively when it is known what is going to happen to the group after the merger. This conviction will be further strengthened if solutions are considered which have been found to work in practice. In any case, the principles of the existing conventional organization theory do not bring us much further than the deployment of a superabundance of managers in a rather artificially contrived top structure specially designed for the situation. (This subject is dealt with more extensively in pages 141–150.)

Nevertheless, this desire to get the management question settled at an early stage is understandable. When a merger is contemplated, everyone involved is concerned about his post-merger position in the new group. This anxiety increases if the talks and negotiations are vague and the structure of the merger process unclear. (The most dangerous moment in the life of a merger is, therefore, the time when decisions have to be made on this point.) Being human inevitably means having certain sensibilities and anxieties about one's own well-being and ideals. When one has to face the consequences of what one has—either rashly or without clearly seeing what the merger will imply—undertaken, it is always possible that those concerned may suddenly, with a shock, come up against a situation they have never wanted and never will want. This need not mean that the work done so far has been in vain. Certainly, the investigation into the purposes of the merger has lessened the risk of a failure after any contract has been signed. It will also mean that confidence increases and that the talks and negotiations are being increasingly replaced by real co-operation. Lastly, the work has not been wasted because, if the merger offered no real opportunities, a timely end has now been put to the adventure.

COMMENT 8, STAGE 20–x-y. UNIFICATION OF MANAGEMENT

It is not always realized that, after the contract has been signed and the merger announced, an intricate pattern of activities must be carried out before the group can really be modified. The period required for this varies from one case to another. However, it is inadvisable, and may even be very dangerous, to change part of a company when it is impossible to change other sectors closely connected with it.

Once a change has been set in motion it cannot be reversed. Moreover, any change sets off a chain reaction, some of which can be foreseen, but parts of which will always defy any powers of forecasting.

There is a very real risk that a process of changes started too soon, or a cycle of alterations begun in the wrong place will, within a short time, lead to a complete disruption of management. The controlled growth towards a new unity will dissolve into chaos and several years will be lost. Worse, the chaos will cause personnel to leave at moments which are often very unfortunate for the company —and regrettably it is seldom the unsatisfactory employees who wish to leave.

During this second part of the merger process, structure and planning are just as important as they are during the first part, although the possible negative results are quite different.

COMMENT 9, ACTIVITY 21–23. UNIFICATION OF ACCOUNTING SYSTEM; FINANCIAL ADMINISTRATION

It is never too early to set up such an administrative system so that the firms which, up till that moment, have led separate lives, are brought under common control. The situation which will arise if this does not succeed, is completely disastrous. This point is stressed because the realization of one central administration with overall control requires time. Moreover, the network plan clearly shows that all the changes which are desirable must wait until this unification has been achieved.

In practice, people are not always so patient. They may find, perhaps six months later, that it is impossible to form an opinion based on figures about the actual course of affairs in the combined companies. Years are needed to repair the damage caused in this way, and there is a definite risk that the merger may fail.

To realize an overall administrative control is a very considerable task demanding great expertise, a large amount of capital to carry through alterations in organization and the ability to keep in view the connection between companies which, in reality, are still only loosely connected.

COMMENT 10, ACTIVITY 21–26. CENTRAL PLANNING

Central planning may be just as essential as central administration. Planning progress control, reporting and information, the figures of the central accounts department and an adequate control of profitability and liquidity will eventually have to be brought together in one central control system.

It seems a tremendous task to achieve all this before the new structure becomes a reality. In a great many cases, however, it is a vital condition for success. The risk that the management will lose its grip on the company is a very real one.

COMMENT 11, ACTIVITY 27–28. ESTABLISHMENT OF OPERATIONAL CONTROL

This comment should be read in connection with, and following on, Comments 9 and 10.

What happens in a merger? The new management consists of one or more ex-colleagues of the working company executives, of outsiders, or a combination of both. In any case, the management will—certainly at first—have to rely on its own, mainly personal authority. Some of the existing directors of the working companies may possibly disagree with the appointment of the group directors. The main board, and possibly the shareholders may take the line that they should wait and see how matters go.

During this first period, therefore, the position of the new management is generally not strong.

Businessmen being only human, it must be recognized that, as the merger progresses, the new group management will only be able to hold its own if in some way it can really take charge. Apart from personal authority, there is no better means of obtaining authority than to have reliable information at one's disposal.

In a sense, therefore, the group management may be saved by the grace of a good information and control system. If there is anything wrong with this system, the management will have a very hard time, and may even come to grief, during the early critical period.

This risk cannot be incurred, for the company itself might also perish along with the management. Therefore, the creation of a good central control system is a critical point which must be rounded before the group can emerge in its new identity.

A TYPICAL QUESTIONNAIRE

During the preliminary talks (Activity 1–2 in the plan) it is of the utmost importance to concentrate on a few main points. This will force partners to form a clear idea of their preliminary conditions and aims.

It may be useful to have a list of questions and to discuss these, point by point, until provisional conclusions can be set down.

Sometimes parts of the questions cannot yet be discussed by the full committee. Even so, it is still useful for the participants to localize these points and form their own opinion on them.

Such a list will include different subjects in different situations. The following list is one which on various occasions has been found satisfactory.

AIMS

1 What aims do partners have in mind with the merger? To what extent are these considerations defensive, or may they be deemed progressive or possibly even aggressive?

2 Are there specific problems in the individual companies or in the group companies as such (no successor, insufficient means to realize a desirable growth, a surplus of cash for which there is no adequate use, too small or too large product ranges, insufficient research and development on raw materials, products or production methods, etc.)?

3 What, in the opinion of partners, may be expected of the developments in their branch of industry (not only in their own country) during the next five or ten years?

4 In connection with these questions, what importance do they attach to the merger with regard to:

   (a) Sales levels achieved so far.
   (b) Product ranges, brands, sales methods, etc.
   (c) Production facilities.
   (d) Staff and personnel.

5 What are the investment plans of partners for the next few years (including the commercial and administrative sectors)?

VALUE AND AUTHORITY IN THE NEW GROUP

1 Should the authority be based on the proportionate value of the companies?

2 Will the valuation of the various companies determine the proportionate value of the whole; or is there any preference for certain loan capital, additional consideration, mutual purchase and sale of shares, etc.?

3 What relative valuations would still be acceptable to the parties, given equal votes or limitation of voting power (e.g. by means of different classes of shares or shareholders' contracts)?

4 Would a take-over also be considered?

5 What importance is attached to the marketability of shares?

6 Are there any compelling conditions as to places on the board or in management?

7 Do the companies possess objects or advantages which are difficult to estimate? (E.g. growth potential, patents and licences, speculative land, special historic circumstances, etc.)

FINANCIAL-LEGAL STRUCTURE

1 Is a new holding company to be created, will one of the existing companies be promoted to the position of holding company, or will the existing working companies become the holders of shares in a new working company and transfer their trading assets into this new company?

2 Would a merger by means of a partnership between individuals and/or companies be a possibility?

3 Would any form of partial merging—for instance a joint venture—be considered?

4 Should parts of the companies or their capital remain outside the merger?

5 Are there to be ordinary shares, A shares, Preference shares, Deferred shares, Non-voting shares; and are voting agreements between shareholders or similar arrangements in the Articles of Association necessary or desirable, e.g. in order to maintain for the present the private or family nature of a company, etc.?

6 What rights are attached to the various shares (appointments, alterations in the Articles of Association, etc.)?

FINANCIAL AND TAXATION CONSIDERATIONS

1 How can Capital Gains Tax be minimized?
2 What taxation warranties are required from the parties?
3 What are the obligations regarding dividends, etc., in the partner companies? (dividends, directors' remuneration, retirement or consultancy provisions, or obligations not reflected in the balance sheet, etc.)
4 What are the dividend requirements for the future?
5 Are there possibilities of strengthening the financial position of the partner companies, or do any of them wish to lessen their financial stake in the combined company?

STRUCTURE AT THE TOP

1 How many directors on the main board are there to be. Should the board consist of the boards of the original companies, or should it be entirely new. Should the division of authority according to shareholdings be carried through to board level. Do partners wish to differentiate between the initial position and future arrangements, or is the board question to be settled once and for all. What will be the age limits and remuneration?
2 Similar questions must be applied to executive management.
3 What control will the shareholders have over the main board, and what control will the main board have over the boards of subsidiaries?
4 What will be the salaries, bonuses, pensions, expense accounts; what is to be done about any fringe benefits (house, use of company staff cars, etc.)?

PERSONNEL

1 Do systems of remuneration (including profit sharing, savings schemes, pension schemes, holiday bonuses, etc.) and ancillary conditions of employment vary much from one company to another?
2 How many people does the executive management of the partner firms comprise; what fields do they cover and is it advisable that they should take part in the merger talks?

3 What will personnel be told during the negotiation period if questions are asked concerning the planned co-operation?

4 Are difficulties anticipated—especially with regard to higher personnel—if the merger plans were to become known or if the merger itself should be announced?

GENERAL

1 A number of operations will have to be set under way concurrently in order that the merger talks may progress with speed. These can best be undertaken by committees, but who will serve on these committees and who should be the chairmen?

2 Are there any requirements, desires or conditions with regard to the name of the new concern. Are there any dangers attached to a common action under one name?

3 Are there other special demands, e.g. concerning succession in the partner companies, the position of relatives, maintaining old business connections (banks, professional advisers, suppliers and so on), special provisions, etc.?

EXAMPLE OF AN ACTION PLAN

The activity (5–6) of quantifying the action plan is included in the network plan.

As has been seen, the purposes of the merger determine the depth of the different parts of the company plan. In general, of course, the greatest detail is required at the point where the merger must produce the biggest results.

For instance, for a merger which aims especially at complementing product ranges, an extensive analysis of turnover, prices, sales channels, promotion and advertising policy is needed, to obtain an insight into the way the new production range must be handled and decide whether one or more commercial organizations should be established. If the latter, there is also the important question of a division of tasks between the sales departments. There are several possible arrangements for this.

In other cases (particularly in the chemical industry) the research and development of new products and production methods is essential. Here the programmes of partners will have to be compared in great detail to see what form the combined activities will take,

also to decide who will undertake certain parts of the nev.
gramme after the merger.

In many cases a merger should bring a fall in production costs.
Many mergers lead to larger budgets for sectors outside production,
because commercial expansion or an extension of research and
development are considered desirable.

This, added to the actual merger costs and the increase in overheads generally brought about by the re-organization, creates a
strong urge to rationalize production. This can only be attained if
we can analyse the way in which the orders the production capacity
has to meet are spread over the various production departments in
the various companies. This knowledge can then be applied to the
new situation.

In this way, possibilities of combining or specializing, of profitable
investments on the basis of a bigger production volume, can be
found.

Once such an analysis is available, the main outlines of the new
production set-up will almost automatically become clear. A
production plan including forecasts of wastage, staffing, productive
employment of machines and departments can then be drawn up
and is essential if the production apparatus is to be quickly adapted
to the new situation.

The plan is just as essential as the basis for an investment plan.
It will show what machines, or groups of machines, will be superfluous, and in which sectors investments will have to be made to
build up a well-balanced plant. The first step in these activities
presents a big problem, for a survey must be obtained of dissimilar
firms with totally different systems of gathering and drawing up
their data.

CALCULATED MERGING

THE ACTION PLAN

A co-ordinated action does not consist of a series of separate
measures in the various areas covered by the merger. It is, rather, a
technical operation built up from a number of mutually sustaining
actions. It needs an action plan based on a vision embodying
numerous aspects of the new combination.

In practice, it is difficult to draw up an effective action plan. If one aims at quick progress, there is a risk that important possibilities may be neglected and others rashly undertaken. The management of the new concern often consists of directors of the original companies who, at first, know little about anything apart from their own company, so that an overall vision is difficult to get. If a 'wait and see' attitude is adopted in order to avoid precipitate action, there is a good chance that opportunities will be missed and that competing companies may carry out counter-moves before the new concern has developed. To find the happy medium and make the right choice from all the possible ways of action needs great skill and judgement.

When one sees with how much thought, care and—mainly financial—statistics the financial and legal structure is built up, one may well wonder at the emotional character which frequently attends action plans, and the small support—in the shape of non-financial business data and calculations—given to businessmen in developing these plans, e.g. data concerning the technical exchangeability of machines and spare parts, raw materials, semi-manufactures and finished products; output and employment figures, and fluctuations in these figures; the size of series, quality requirements; size, kind and composition of orders.

The lack of exact business data and calculation in the foundations for an action plan is dangerous for without them it is impossible to obtain a specific insight into the potential advantages of a merger. There is, for instance, a considerable chance that, after the merger, those sectors will first be combined which can be easily understood and managed, but that others which might offer greater advantages are too long left out of account, because they cannot be discovered without an analysis in depth. An action plan which is not founded on exact data, frequently falls down on the very sectors where the effect of the merger is hard to forecast intuitively. These will hardly be mentioned in the action plan and possible advantages of the merger will only be realized much later, or not at all.

For instance, where a general insurance and life assurance company were merged, it was found that the advantages were caused not so much by amalgamating the administration of the two companies, but by combining the outside activities, something which neither of the—widely different—companies had foreseen. The reverse may also be true. Without sufficient understanding of a certain sector it may be given undue prominence in the action plan and—after incurring great cost in realizing the merger—disappointment ensues.

It is, therefore, most important to analyse systematically those sectors where potential is not sufficiently clear when the action plan is drawn up. By methodically gathering and linking the business data it will become clear whether or not amalgamation would offer advantages and if so, how they could be realized. In this way, the action plan will gain the same reliability which underlies the financial and legal structure based on the reports of financial and/or legal advisers.

INFLUENCE OF ACTION PLAN ON DECISION TO MERGE

Although execution of the action plan cannot normally begin until the merger has become a fact, there may be great advantages in starting work on the plan in the early stages of the negotiations. If work on the plan is only begun after the signing of the merger, time will be lost, or actions undertaken without full understanding of the consequences. Both situations can be avoided if part of the—often lengthy—negotiation period is used to lay the groundwork for a well-documented action plan.

Even more important is the argument that insight obtained by working on a definite action plan may have considerable influence on the decision to merge. On the one hand, merger talks sometimes break down because there is no clear understanding of the possible advantages and parties do not wish to risk their future on vague expectations. On the other hand, they are sometimes concluded on the basis of optimistic—albeit not very clear—expectations, and parties later find that these expectations were largely illusory. In such cases, the definite prospects furnished by a systematic analysis of 'hazy' sectors, carried out with a view to the action plan, may help the negotiations over a critical phase and also warn against rash steps.

Great confidence between the merging groups is, of course, required to exchange the data needed for the analysis before the merger agreement has been signed, but this is a matter of 'fair exchange' and often no one will be in a privileged position. The worst that can happen is that negotiating parties together will come to occupy a stronger position *vis-à-vis* their competitors by knowing details about each other which these competitors do not know. In certain cases an independent third party can be called in to bridge the gap by handling confidential information prior to business data being exchanged, in order that the development of an action plan may not be delayed.

The systematic analysis of business sectors which is to help the businessman in developing his action plan, may take various forms. Sometimes, an examination of the organizational structure and staffing of certain sectors of the merging companies is the first step. In other cases, an inventory is taken of plant and premises. Occasionally, products are compared with a view to standardization.

In practice, an analysis of the combined orders of the merging companies may, especially for industrial companies, provide an answer to a great many of the questions arising when different business sectors are joined. Such a survey can be made once all the orders executed by the merging companies over a recent period have been analysed. For this, all the orders executed by these companies during, say, the latest full financial year, must be listed according to different aspects:

1 Type of product.
2 Sales channel.
3 Consumer group.
4 Time of arrival, specification or classification.
5 Time of delivery.
6 Demand made on means of production.
7 Extent to which order could be combined with other orders in the production sector.
8 Raw materials required, sub-divided as to quality.

To obtain comparable results, partners must agree beforehand the classification of products, sales channels, consumer groups, means of production, production departments, etc. The data is coded so that uniform treatment for punchcard or for computer analysis is possible.

It is clear that these talks will afford partners some measure of understanding of each other's firms. This will facilitate later discussions of the results. The results of this analysis, on thousands of punchcards, will take shape as the analysis provides accurate answers to all kinds of questions surrounding the integration of the merging companies, and so provide a definite basis for the action plan.

Seasonal fluctuations in orders of various groups of products can now for instance be determined within a few hours. Figure 4 shows the answer to such a question. The year has been divided into 10 periods; the products to be supplied, per period, categories I, II and III, are shown vertically.

Product category I is more prone to seasonal fluctuations, which may give rise to the question whether this part of the total production would still be profitable for the new company. By comparing this graph with similar graphs of each of the merging companies— which can, of course, be drawn up just as easily—we can see to what extent a more even production flow could be achieved by a merger.

Other punchcard operations may yield an insight into the

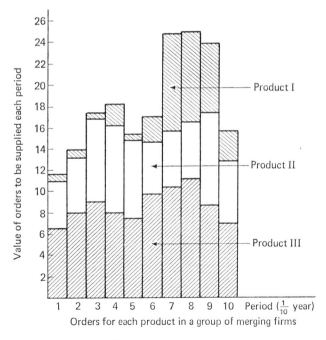

Fig. 4. The result of an order analysis.

possibilities of combining orders in the purchasing or sales departments. Sales of the various products for each type of customer are also interesting. These can be compared with national statistics, so that the share in the market of the various companies can be calculated and an impression obtained of the completeness of the range of articles.

The systematic order analysis provides an insight into various sections of an industrial enterprise which it would be difficult to obtain in a comparatively short time in any other way. Once the data has been registered on punchcards it can be used in a great many ways. This makes the method efficient, for the coded data is used more than once.

THE ACTION PLAN IN THE PRODUCTION SECTOR

An order analysis is particularly useful in investigations into the production sector of merging companies to check possibilities of reducing costs. If one aims to reduce costs, the greater part of this reduction will have to be obtained by rationalizing production. Cutting costs by means of more rational production will do more towards strengthening the combination than an improvement in the company's position on the buying and selling market; a position which is frequently based on commercial/political power factors which—no matter how important—are often of a temporary nature.

In a mixed business with a wide range of products and means of production, possibilities in the production sector are far from clear. In mergers of these companies, opportunities in the production processes are often overshadowed by the purchasing and sales sectors. This is a pity, because in this type of company the output of many groups of machines remains low and considerable improvements in the average productive use of machines could be effected by a merger.

An improvement in productive use can usually not be realized without a re-grouping of some of the plant of the partner companies. This cannot be done 'experimentally', but must be set forth in a detailed and well-thought-out action plan. All the phases of the re-grouping are closely linked, and the first phases cannot begin until all the consecutive phases have been planned.

If the order analysis is so arranged, the calculation of machine capacity needed after the merger can be quite simple. If the use of groups of machines per order has been accurately registered on the punchcards, one can trace exactly how they have affected the employment of a certain group of machines during the year.

As an example, Figure 5 shows the use, during the year, of a certain kind of loom employed in the mills of two weaving companies planning a merger. Horizontally, the year is divided into ten periods; vertically, required deliveries for each period are shown in millions of 'picks'. Each period has been sub-divided according to the time when the orders were placed. From this, it is possible to calculate the extent to which orders can be produced before the delivery date in order to obtain a more even employment of the group of machines.

In the graph, this calculation results in the horizontal broken line, which shows the required production capacity for each period. This means that the peaks in delivery need not be carried through

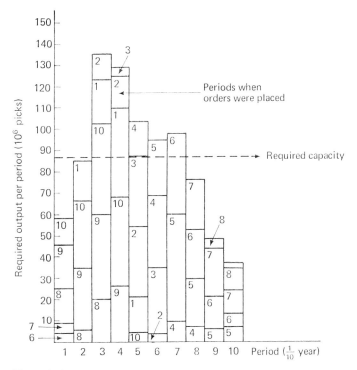

Fig. 5. Order analysis for the production sector of merging weaving-mills. Note that numbers indicate periods when orders were placed.

into the mills, but can be ironed out by finishing the booked orders in time and according to plan. As might be expected, these graphs often show that the combined production of merging companies requires a smaller capacity than the total required by the original companies.

In this way, we can approximate the effect of amalgamating the orders of the merging companies, and the required machine capacity can thus be found, expressed in product quantities. At the same time, the whole production sector becomes so clear that an exact re-grouping plan is now possible. As every sales forecast can now be quickly and easily translated into its consequences for the factory, considerable progress has also been made in connecting the commercial and technical side of the action plan, which is one of the main problems in a merger.

BETTER CHANCES THROUGH CALCULATED MERGING

As the example of an order analysis shows, it is possible to base the action plan on definite business statistics. Apart from the order analysis, there are various other methods which, for different types of company and different problems, may be useful. In every case, the method chosen must always be the one that will best serve its purpose—an action plan which is effective and reliable and can quickly be realized.

The financial and legal structure of a merger provides the security and a chance to develop. The action plan must be the focal point during the stage following successful negotiations: the integration of a number of separate businesses into one strong entity. This lends the work on an action plan a meaning far beyond that of simply drawing up a plan.

Obviously, in a merger, close co-operation between the partners is essential. It must bridge differences in mental approach and will finally result in completely unanimous action in the interests of the new concern. At the top this is an especially difficult task, demanding great mental effort and self-sacrifice, for the interests of the new concern will not always run parallel to the personal interests of all the managers. The personal sacrifices made in the interests of the future concern may not always be spectacular, but are no less hard for that.

Personal feelings among partners and the uncertainty which

almost always attends a merger, will, however, weigh less heavily if directors and managers of the merging companies can co-operate in an action plan which is based on impartial figures. The subtle interplay of move and counter-move is then replaced by a co-operation aimed at expanding the whole and not at maintaining one's own position within that whole. The equal exchange of data provides a feeling of security and the partners, once rivals, will gradually begin to develop a common vision of the new concern, at a rate which could never be reached by discussing valuations, key positions, forms of management, etc., however important these may be.

In this way, the work on a definite action plan, like the work on the financial and legal structure, provides an essential contribution to the growth of a merger, for thoughts are thus turned to future expansion, and the rate at which the advantages of the merger are realized is thus greatly increased.

VALUATION OF COMPANIES ON A SHARE EXCHANGE BASIS

Thinking on the subject of valuation varies widely, not only from country to country, but also from individual to dividual. To some, profits potential is the main criterion, to others the underlying assets value and so on.

Valuation is a basic part of the merger process. It is not simply a matter of bringing in a professional valuer, who may appear to produce a valuation of the companies involved, somewhat miraculously. Valuation is often thought of as a kind of accountants' trick, whereas it is simply an appreciation of how the assets and earnings capacity of the company can be used to its greatest potential. It is not enough for the directors to hand the problem over to the expert valuer: they must be concerned at all stages of the valuation that full weight is given to all the factors, of which they, and only they are fully informed.

This is not intended to be a detailed exposition on valuation. The aim is to provide those involved in a merger with the basic outline principles and approaches and alternative methods of valuation, so that they may be able to instruct and co-operate with their professional advisers as to the precise factors they should take into account in valuing the businesses concerned, having regard to the particular use to which assets and earning capacity are currently put and will be put following the merger.

For the British or American company, the dominant factor in valuation is the future earning capacity, or even turnover, of the merged group. Although it is evident that this is also the starting point for many continental companies, it is so influenced by other considerations, particularly net assets values, that on the face of things it appears that there are many different methods of valuation that are seemingly incompatible. The criteria upon which valuations are based vary widely from country to country, and even within countries.

The main reasons for this are: the disguise of profits or losses in published accounts; the disguise of profits in view of traditional attitudes *vis à vis* fiscal authorities; many family-owned firms delay co-operation until it is too late, when there are losses and only the buyer's efforts will restore profitability. Asset valuation has become so habitual that even profitable firms are valued more by assets than by profit potential. Therefore in certain cases, British companies have purchased continental companies on the basis of earnings capacity which, although justified by normal UK practice, meant that they paid more for the companies than they need have done.

BASES OF VALUATION

1 DISCOUNTED CASH FLOW. By discounted cash flow, not only is value of earnings taken into account, but also the capital investment programme required to achieve them. The major practical difficulties in its application are what discounting rates should be used, and at what time will technological developments require that modernization of plant be initiated. The full potential of this method of valuation has not yet been realized anywhere in the world.

2 EARNINGS BASIS. A company's earnings value in this method is expressed by multiplying its net profit by a chosen number of years (the P/E Ratio) to give its capital value. The main problems with this method of valuation are:

A: How should the net earnings be computed?

B: How many years purchase should be taken?

A: DETERMINATION OF NET EARNINGS

In practice there are several methods we can choose from, some of
which are as follows:

1 THE HISTORICAL METHOD. For this, the earnings shown by
   the audited profit and loss accounts over a number of years
   are averaged according to a certain formula either a simple
   or weighted average. This method has the advantage of being
   based on established figures, but the disadvantage of giving too
   much attention to the past.

2 THE ADJUSTED HISTORICAL METHOD. Here the profit and
   loss account is amended to take account of changes in circumstances, e.g. availability and variations in the price of labour
   (wages and proprietor/directors' remuneration and benefits),
   the quantities of raw materials and the hours of labour usage,
   selling prices and depreciation, obsolescence, capital expenditure charged to revenue, and variations in taxation, direct and
   indirect, and interest rates.

3 THE METHOD OF PROFIT POTENTIAL. An assessment is
   made of likely future earnings, taking account, not only of
   current circumstances, but also the improved skills of management and other factors available to the company when
   merged.

B: HOW MANY YEAR'S PURCHASE SHOULD BE TAKEN?

The first method derived from interest theory, used mainly on the
Continent, puts the yield required at the level of interest of so-called
gilt-edged securities. This is largely academic.

Against this, it is considered that the yield on equities is a
better comparison. There is something to be said for the idea that
the yield must be taken from the average of the group of companies to which the company belongs rather than the *Financial
Times* Actuaries Index as a whole. It is as yet hardly possible to
evaluate these opinions and the choice will generally be a matter
for negotiation.

A completely different distinction arises in the question of whether
the profit (net return) should be capitalized before or after taxation.

Important points here are the legal structure of the companies and the taxes which have been paid so far.

ASSETS BASIS

When property is valued it is of great importance to find out what standards are applied in determining its value. The market value with vacant possession is often far higher than when occupied.

PLANT AND EQUIPMENT

Starting-points are the going concern, the market and the adjusted book values. As a going concern, the plant is valued on the present and future technical and economic usefulness of the machines without regard to age. Opinions vary widely as to when market value should be used. In valuations carried out with a view to merging, a problem arises in cases where the oldest part of the plant will become 'superfluous' simply because of the merger. For a company which does not consist entirely of very old or the most modern machines, the starting-point of the adjusted book value offers a reasonable mean.

VALUATION OF STOCK

With regard to stock there are two fundamentally different opinions —valuation on the basis of *market value* and valuation on the basis of *costs*. As profit margins may vary, different bases produce different results. There is also the question of valuing unmarketable stock. There may be a considerable difference in determining the point beyond which goods are regarded as unmarketable.

VALUATION OF INTANGIBLE ASSETS

For intangible assets, the intrinsic value can really only be determined for patents, licences or other rights which have been either acquired or developed. It is very tempting to value these items according to their earning power. Other standards can, however, be considered, e.g.:

1 A combination of costs and the period of usefulness. This may
   be judged either on a time or piece basis.
2 The sales value if the patents or licences are marketable.
3 An estimate of the extra costs which would have to be incurred
   if one did not possess the patent or licence.

Other factors to be considered include: the assessment of pension
rights and other liabilities; tax losses; claims under service contracts; redundancy pay; guarantees.

4 Assets plus goodwill (based on earnings). Here a capitalized value of (super-) earnings is combined with the assets
   value of the company. An investigation is required to find out
   whether the profits are higher or lower than the required
   yield (see earnings basis) on a capital that equals the assets
   value. The difference capitalized is indicated as the (positive
   or negative) goodwill.

BARGAINING FACTORS

One factor which will considerably affect the final valuation is
where one company is a major customer of the other. The extent
to which the profitability of the supplier can be ascribed to that
firm is a matter for negotiation.

Acquiring a majority of the shares. If a big shareholder, for
instance, wishes to acquire a majority of shares, a block of shares
which will bump up the holding to effective control, may be of
infinite value. Clearly, this value does not depend on the asset or
the earnings value of that small block of shares. The reverse may
occur for those shareholders who have no (or hardly any) influence
on the course of affairs in a company, unless there are special factors
affecting minority holders.

MANAGEMENT STRUCTURE

Quite often, the management structure is discussed either at the
beginning or at the very end of the merger talks. The determination
of the top structure is hardly ever regarded as the key factor from
which drive and initiative is to flow.

It is most important to realize that there is a relationship between the determination of the top structure and of development plans, financial/legal structure and even of the valuation. If the problem is analysed at the time when these points are discussed, it will be clear what the requirements for the top structure in a merger must be.

STRUCTURE OF TOP MANAGEMENT IN MERGERS

INTRODUCTION

There are a number of different reasons for taking a closer look at the problems of the structure of top management in mergers.

1 The fact that many mergers are planned to come into being rapidly is a problem. Talks may be held up, and even fail, because agreement cannot be reached on the size of the management and the division of tasks between the various managers.

2 A merger often presents great human difficulties for executives. These problems may arise out of an inability to cope with the new situation. They may, however, also be caused by a struggle for power, which gradually begins to reveal itself.

3 At least as dangerous is the fact that the realization of mergers is sometimes delayed, or fails completely, because a top executive 'blocks' some part of the company which should produce a considerable part of the profit of the merger. Mostly, it then becomes obvious that the executive concerned is unable to conform to the new policy required after the merger. This may not be due to obstinacy but may be a result of previously holding a responsible position. He may have become so wedded to his ideas and opinions that he is unable to do things differently.

There follows an explanation of a number of the reasons for these difficulties and an indication of ways in which they might perhaps be solved. It must, however, be stressed that this is no more than a first approach to the problem.

In a take-over (as opposed to a merger) there are rarely any insuperable problems. During the initial period, the parent company frequently leaves the existing management intact and awaits developments. Gradually it begins to lay down a few directives and standards. If it does not succeed in bringing the subsidiary into line, someone from head office is brought in and added to the existing management. If there are still difficulties, then some or even all, of the original directors may be transferred, or may be dismissed with or without a golden handshake. Although the human distress this entails should not be under-estimated, the continuity and the purposes of the company are rarely seriously threatened by problems arising from the structure at the top. In other words, in a take-over one hardly ever arrives at a deadlock. The necessary measures have been taken before this occurs.

This is also the case in mergers of large and very large companies. In these, it is much easier to transfer directors. Also, the directors of large companies are far more accustomed to being moved from one place to another, sometimes at very short notice. They can more easily and rapidly adapt themselves to a new task or a new situation. In addition, the alterations due to increase in size are far less drastic for a large company than they are for smaller and medium-sized firms. The adaptability required from management is therefore less in a big company than it is in medium-sized and small companies.

This, however, does not mean that phenomena such as a struggle for power or an inability to cope with new positions, do not occur in big companies. In fact, they have often occurred there before. People are used to them and able to deal with them and have some experience in solving this kind of problem.

Because the consequences of such problems are greatest in the sector of the smaller and medium-sized companies, and the systematic accumulation and exchange of experience least, it is most relevant to restrict discussion to this type of concern.

SURPLUS OF DIRECTORS

Although mergers have generally occurred more often in large concerns than in smaller companies, they have recently been spreading to medium-sized and smaller companies, and it seems likely that during the next few years mergers will increasingly take place in this sector.

In medium-sized (mostly family) companies and in most smaller firms the management is entrusted to more than one director. Although the size of the company created by a merger of medium-sized concerns is rarely such as to require more than two or three senior directors, it is, in practice, almost always agreed that the present positions of directors shall be maintained. It will be obvious how such a unanimous opinion is reached without going into the emotions and prestige considerations involved. It is relatively unimportant whether this situation evolves from some kind of mutual consultation, or whether it is the result of instructions to an adviser, including a number of conditions which, in effect, mean that the present positions must, as far as possible, be maintained.

Conventional organization theory also provides techniques for breaking down the quantity of work according to kind and nature, space and time, into the minutest components, and then to re-structure them.

One or two principles may have to be violated on account of compromise, but finally a picture emerges in which everyone has his place. The result, after the merger, is practically always a company with too many managers. An attempt to solve this problem by the appointment of some weak committee is often made.

The impotence inherent in such a situation frequently leads to prolonged effort to retain what the merged companies had already achieved in the market, and at the same time to desperate but not very fruitful attempts to realize the new plans. At the worst, a struggle for power will then ensue, which will result in a reconstruction at the top with effective management being limited to one man or just a few. Such cases may even be fatal to the merger, and the merged concern will become a cheap acquisition for a larger competitor.

MERGERS AND A SHORTAGE OF DIRECTORS

A merger means an increase in scale. Instead of gradual normal growth, there is a sudden expansion which frequently amounts to twice or three times the size. At first, this increase exists only on paper, for just after the merger the companies themselves are hardly altered. The enterprises are only connected by means of the signatures of the shareholders, and/or directors on contracts.

If this were all, the problems of realizing the merger would be easily solved. However, this is not the case. A merger almost always arises from the desire of the merged companies to produce a new unit. This new company is to produce at lower costs, or to obtain a new position on the market, or to form a concentration of power with which new objectives may be achieved.

Take the case of a three-company merger—instead of three forms of policy, one new policy must now be evolved. In other words, by means of a total re-organization, one unit will emerge which will in no way be comparable to any one of the three original, nor to the three combined companies immediately after the merger. This means a host of changes both internally—in the extent and the nature of the processes which together form the company—and externally in the actions of the company.

In this connection, a re-division of the activities which were already carried on seems obvious, but a far more essential task will be to scrap certain activities and to undertake completely new ones. In consequence, other talents will be needed to lead the merged concern than were required in the separate companies prior to the merger.

A merger also means a change of emphasis in management problems. There is a tendency for existing connections to be cut and new ones created. What is stressed now is not good, efficient and 'cost-conscious' management of one sector, but the forceful realization of a clearly defined aim (e.g. carrying out a re-distribution programme for machines or integrating administrations, realizing commercial expansion plans). It is clear these cannot be derived from former functions; importance, content and nature of the work differ too widely.

The increase in scale has another consequence. Before the merger, the independent companies presented essentially different images to the world. If a merger is to succeed, these diverging personalities must, within the shortest time, be transformed into one new personality. A particularly strong personality is required to see that these efforts do not get bogged down in half-heartedness and compromise.

For the managing director of any of the original companies, this role is absolutely impossible for, in the smaller companies, work is hardly ever carried out according to instructions or directions derived from a written policy. Rightly or wrongly, the business is what the management says and does. Such a managing director would, even if he understood the new policy, first have to change himself to guide the new unit.

Finally, a completely different factor which generally attends a merger is that realization of the aims must for preference be carried out within the shortest possible time. From the moment the merger is announced, the new concern is particularly vulnerable (see also pages 153–156). This means that under the pressure of these special circumstances, a number of drastic changes must take place at a rate at which none of the companies has experience.

The increase in scale, the new policy, the greatly increasing dynamism and the altered standards of management mean that—although there is almost always a surplus of directors—there is at the same time a shortage of management meeting the specific requirements for a successful realization of the merger. This is not a matter of whether the present managements are good or bad; it is simply because, with the merger, all the executives of the different companies have been transferred to a new concern in one sweep. In this there is no longer room for the individualistic approach of the managing director of a smaller company; a new approach is required.

This simultaneous surplus and shortage of directors forms the key problem which must be solved in structuring top management in a merger.

FAILURE OF THE CONVENTIONAL ORGANIZATION THEORY

A characteristic of the conventional organization theory is the assumption of a certain calmness to observe the processes required for any given purpose, to analyse them into component parts for action, and then to discover the optimum grouping according to quantity, nature and level. The calmness, too, during a fairly lengthy period to carry out the regrouping which as 'target structure' will produce some idea of a working pattern more satisfactory than the present one. Thus, there is a 'growth towards' a certain development.

It is recognized that this theory may lead to a rather rigid organization. In practice, it has proved more fruitful for those organizations which are not (or only gradually) subject to change.

If changes take place too rapidly, it seems likely that the necessary calm will be lacking and, even worse, that the task—the very basis of the system—will no longer offer a firm hold, for obviously the possibilities of using the conventional organization theory disappear as operations and working patterns change more rapidly than the time required to draw up a target structure. Or, to put it differently: as soon as the pattern of aims of the business is subject to continual change, the conventional organization theory falls down.

This is increasingly the case. The changes in society nowadays are such that the pattern of aims *must* change continually, if it is not to lag behind. The merger is a symptom of these changes. To include a full description of the development of society would take us too far afield. Suffice it to say that this development involves an increasing dynamism, often requires an accelerated growth and increases the demands made on management, decision-making and adaptability. For many companies, these changes mean the end of quiet development—and with it tranquillity at the top.

The company can no longer be regarded as a separate entity but must be set and analysed in the context of, and as a reaction to, the entire social development. The establishment of the identity of the group is a primary condition. Understanding of social development is an essential secondary condition. The dynamism of society must be countered by the flexibility of the company. For this kind of 'controlled' reaction, the division of working processes into tasks, responsibilities and powers will have to be made subordinate to arranging the changes the company will have to undergo.

The heart of the company's development problem is found in the structure of the movements towards a (probably) Final plan. This is very different from manipulating the activities of a great number of directors, in order to fit them into a structure which will later prove to have no real strength but only to maintain the outward appearance of an existing status.

STRUCTURE OF TOP MANAGEMENT IN A MERGER

If a merger remains merely a legal entity, the constituent companies continue to function as they did before and the calm required to realize a gradual, sometimes almost imperceptible, amalgamation returns. This seldom happens.

The ideas are, therefore, based on a combination of companies which, after the merger, have to develop rapidly and with sweeping alterations into a completely new concern. In this context one may think of the integration of production plants (see also pages 129–137) or administration, of the realization of a common research or commercial programme.

There is a clear distinction between two hierarchic levels which usually arise in a merger but generally cannot materially be distinguished as such. These are, on the one hand, the level of management to control the merged companies; on the other, the level of mangements of the existing companies, here referred to as the management of the working companies. We must, however, bear in mind that there is not always a legal distinction between the merged group and the working company levels. This depends on which financial/legal structure has been chosen.

For the *group management*, the most important point is a restriction of the number of members, primarily so that inflation of the board can be avoided, secondly so that the power to make decisions can be maintained in the company. It will frequently be an advantage to appoint at least one member of the group board from outside. It is clear that such a decision is not easily taken. But such a situation —if among the present directors there are no men who are capable of realizing the merger—will greatly decrease the risk of falling profits and capital, struggle for power, failure of all plans, etc.

At the level of the *working company management* a different approach must be taken. Here, one starts not from a situation of calm but from a fluid and changing situation. In order to indicate an alternative to the approach offered by the conventional organization theory, this fluidity must first be made visible. To do this one must go back to the actual merger.

In electing to merge, one has in mind a number of aims in different fields. Some of these may be more important or more urgent to the success of the merger than others. Therefore, it is important for any merger to possess good action or development plans (see also pages 150–161). These plans must provide a coordinated picture of what is to be established in the fields of commerce, production, administration, product development and financing. A well-constructed plan of action for the realization of a merger will, in broad outline, show the changes which the companies will have to undergo during a fairly short period after the formal merger.

The combination of the necessary changes described in the action plans shows what aims are to be achieved in different fields at different times and what the connection is between them. The realization of the purposes forms a network plan which can be set out in the same way as, for instance, the network for the course of activities for the building of any project. (These concepts have been derived from the plan methods of network planning—Critical Path Method and Programme Evaluation and Review Technique.) In the same way as for the planning of a building we can determine the critical path in the planning of the realization of a merger.

We can, therefore, indicate the critical phases and components in an action plan. Sometimes this may be a movement in the production (integration of production plants), sometimes a commercial development (new brands, new markets, etc.). In any case, a good combination of action plans will show what are the essential parts in the process of realizing the merger and the vital points in each part. In this sense, a network is created which shows the purposes to be attained and which is independent of the time factor, to the extent that the sequential nature and the critical parts are shown but not the detailed working times with specific tasks.

When we have, in this way, 'clarified' a merger, it has become possible to base the structure at the top on the purposes indicated by the network. Thus we get a 'project structure' instead of a 'task structure'. This project structure offers far more opportunities to make use of specific capacities than does the task structure. Moreover—and this is highly important—we can see to it that those projects which form part of the critical path in the development plan, are undertaken by people who will be able to realize them.

The result of applying these ideas to management structure will be that, at working company level, a far greater range of possibilities will be created to fit in people from the merged companies. It will also prove possible to lessen the human difficulties without economic sacrifice regarding the speed and effectiveness of the merger.

In this way the management structure—at working company level —is adapted to the demands made by the realization of the merger and not to the number of jobs which must be made available. By a refining of the project structure it also becomes possible to obtain a much larger flexibility in the management of the company and its executives—e.g. adaptation to the time-span of executives (see Elliott Jacques: 'Equitable Payment')—than can ever be possible in a task structure. The critical path shows where concessions cannot be tolerated. An added advantage is that questions of status which are so closely connected with the task structure, are connected with the purpose envisaged in a project structure. In this way, forces are brought into line which, in a task structure, often have a delaying effect.

In this sense, a restriction of the number of directors at group level, and the use of a project structure at working company level, will reduce many of the problems inherent in creating a top management of reasonable proportions.

COMMERCIAL ASPECTS

Agreement on a merger is the beginning of a nerve-racking time. Shares must be issued, Articles of Association altered, appointments made, taxation matters settled—and at the same time a start must be made with definite co-operation, in an atmosphere which is, to say the least, unsettling. Partners will concentrate on the obvious activities and there is a risk that they may forget—although only temporarily—that the merged companies are, in fact, still separately operating companies. The result may be that they immediately stop competing: from now on all will be peace and harmony. The advantages of this attitude will be gained, not by the new concern, but by its competitors who have, no doubt, been alerted by the news of the merger. As this may lead to considerable loss, a separate section is devoted to the cause and prevention of this situation: 'commercial policy in mergers'.

COMMERCIAL POLICY IN MERGERS

EEC AND MERGING

By a merger, we mean the amalgamation of a number of companies, whereby the individual independence of each company up to the moment of the merger disappears to create a larger whole. A new company is born. If the amalgamation of companies is a unilateral event, we would prefer to call it a take-over. For instance, if the contribution of two merging firms, A and B, is in the proportion of ten-to-one, it may be nice for company B to be able to say that it has 'merged' with A. By a merger we understand the amalgamation of more or less equal partners.

The threat which EEC forms to nationally-orientated companies is far from illusory. Mergers may be regarded as a fashionable phenomenon, but anyone who sees just across the frontier, companies in his own industry many times larger than his own has some reason for anxiety. This is all the more justified when it is found that the size needed for future competition with these giants over the border, cannot be realized by normal expansion during the years when the EEC is still in a state of development. In order to ensure the continuation of the company in the EEC-era, the necessary size will have to be otherwise obtained.

The horizontal merger offers a unique means of multiplying the present size of the company. It offers, not only an increase in scale, but also the possibility of a much higher calibre of management. This will open up the way to negotiations with—now equal—companies, which the original partners would hardly have dared to approach at all. There are prospects for an unprecedented rate of growth.

THE SCALE-INCREASING MERGER

The new company born from the merger will quickly have to overcome its childhood disease and adolescence. This rapid growth to adulthood requires a purposeful and effective plan of action. That plan can never be the sum of all that the merger partners had planned to do separately without the merger. The new size of the company presents different problems and different opportunities. Whereas, the partners formerly each had their own equals, the new company finds itself in quite different company. There are new competitors which it must watch, a new policy must be developed, aimed at new objectives.

In production, buying and administration the purposes of the scale-increasing merger are usually clear—rationalization and a reduction in production costs. All kinds of activities may contribute: specialization in processing or products, a levelling-out of fluctuations in employment, mechanization or automation in offices and factory, standardization, normalization. Almost all the changes required in production, administration and purchasing are possible with a technical-mathematical approach. The technical unification of the merger partners can be calculated. This comprises activities in which, apart from specialization, integration and differentiation, a continuous attention to detail, a progressive refining of methods and control of the industrial process will lead to the final goal.

COMMERCIAL SECTOR

All this is very different in the commercial sector! To begin with, economies are generally difficult, while a merger offers a grave risk to sales. No customer likes to be dependent on one supplier. No customer is pleased when a number of competing companies which formerly permitted him to play off one against the other, now present him with a closed front. His natural reaction will be to seek compensation for this blow to his position. This compensation is to be found only from other suppliers.

It has been found that this causes the turnover of the new group to drop unless it makes great commercial efforts. Whether the group of consumers of the merged firms consists of a nameless host of customers or a small group of known specialists, the merger of the original companies suddenly changes their image to their customers. The big question facing the new concern is whether this changed image can be used to form the starting-point of a new expansion, or whether they should passively allow their disappointed customers to turn to other sources and spend their purchasing budgets elsewhere.

CUSTOMER RESPONSE

In his decision to buy, the customer is influenced by the rational and irrational, the real and the unrealistic, the relevant and irrelevant opinions about the company and its products. In the theories of advertising this has led to introduction of the concept of 'image': a chosen picture which is created for a product, brand or company. It is, however, becoming clear that influence by means of advertising can be no more than one factor in forming this image. Even when there is no advertising, there is an 'image' which will affect the decision to buy.

The effect of all the sales efforts, from public relations to the calls of salesmen, of all the suggestions which are in any way projected on to the market, is in the final instance determined by the *subjective shape which the firm as an entity has assumed for the surrounding world*. In this shape, not only the characteristics or the packing of the product, or the way in which it is sold, but everything which permeates from the company to the world outside, plays its part. Therefore, the totality with which we are here concerned, is not fully described by the concept of 'image'. How does this affect the turnover? On the negative side this question is easy to answer. Comparing the company to a human being, some people always present conflicting impressions; the reaction is: 'We don't know where we are with him' and in that case one prefers not to deal with the man. A company, which as an entity presents an illogical, conflicting picture, will repulse first one and then another, and finally all its customers. The public response is not homogeneous: the effect of the sales effort is nil.

It is essential for steady, continuously increasing sales to have a homogenous public response arising, not only from the co-ordination of product, packing and advertising, but also from a consistent policy in every respect—time of delivery (long or short), determination of prices (rigid or opportunistic), business ethics (fundamental or flexible), social climate (soft or hard), buildings (business-like or monumental), investment policy (using things economically or buying the newest), stock exchange (stable or speculative stock).

All sales are the result of the company's attitude as a whole; any sale possessing any continuity at all, is carried by the public response which the firm has, purposely or inadvertently, called up in its customers. Any alterations in this public response will produce an alteration in the sales pattern.

MERGER AND SALES—FIRST PHASE

SEPARATION OF PRODUCTION AND SALES

In scale-increasing mergers, we find a very abrupt alteration in public response if partners immediately combine their sales apparatus. Such precipitate energy may have the result that the loss in turnover (which in any case threatens the concern) becomes fatal. *A rapid and full separation of production and sales in each of the merger partner firms is the best possible remedy for a loss of turnover after the merger.* In the production sector, the first step should be a rationalization, headed by one person, in order to reduce costs. In the commercial sector, on the other hand, this is a time of necessary expansion in many fields, an expansion which will be possible only if the various sales bodies are given a large degree of independence and are, therefore, not headed by one person. The roads of sales and production must diverge.

CENTRAL PLANNING AND A MANAGERIAL DEPARTMENT

The separation of sales and production in the various companies must be followed up in the organization. The most effective and—in spite of psychological obstacles—always feasible measure is the concentration of all sales planning of the companies. In order to bridge the difference in purpose, nature and rate of sales and production, more is required than just central planning. Around this planning we must build up a managerial department to follow the development of production and sales. The task of such a department, it has been found, depends on type of company and the aims of the merger.

SALES BODIES OPERATING INDEPENDENTLY

Figure 6 shows the organizational consequences of the proposed policy. The purpose of the policy must be attained by the now independent sales bodies. Figure 7 gives a simplified picture of this policy, which aims at preventing the possible loss of turnover during the first year after the merger by extra efforts with the existing groups of customers. This can only be achieved by carefully preserving the existing public response to the different companies. For this, the various sales bodies must have a large measure of freedom. If the central planning finds that an order cannot be produced within the time of delivery necessary to obtain the order, the sales bodies must even have powers to farm out the work.

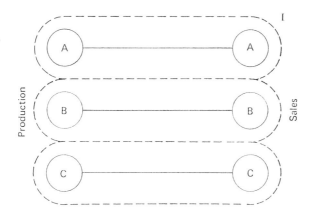

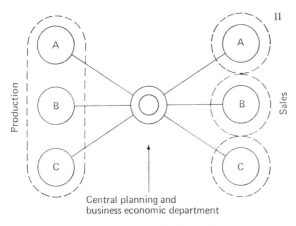

Central planning and
business economic department

Fig. 6. Merger diagram. After the merger of A, B and C, the sales departments are
made independent.

In the production sector, it is often extremely useful to place all the factories under one management immediately. In the commercial sector, the introduction of one central sales management during the first year of the merger is almost always inadvisable. Unlike the production sector, the commercial sector must primarily direct its attention outwards from the existing position; not inwards from a vision of the future.

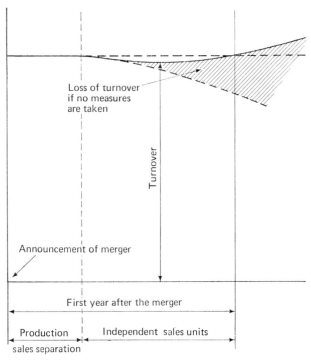

Fig. 7. First phase of merger. During this phase efforts must be made to combat
any possible drop in turnover.

MERGER AND SALES—SECOND PHASE

SHORT-TERM ACTION; LONG-TERM THINKING

During the first year after the merger, while sales and production
departments are separately fighting their initial battles, the newly-
formed group management should immediately after—ideally even
before—the merger, develop the policy which, after the period of
childhood and adolescence, is to bring the concern to adult expansion. The activities immediately after the merger (see pages
153–156) and the development of a long-term policy must be
clearly distinguished.

One can frequently observe the negative results produced by
confusing these two points: long-term thinking produces a loss of

speed in the actions required immediately, but essential long-term thinking is held up by the initial problems. Therefore, in the commercial sector especially, *a functional division between decisive action during the first months and careful thought on the long-term policy must be considered essential.* Although mutual consultation and, perhaps, outside help are useful and necessary, the short-term activities are the direct responsibility of the managers of the various sales bodies, and the development of a long-term policy is primarily the responsibility of the group management.

LONG-TERM POLICY: EXPANSION

The group management has the job of developing a policy of expansion which can be set under way within a year. The consequence of this policy will be a reconstruction of the existing sales departments into a few new units, each with a homogeneous public response. Almost all these new units will have to establish a harmonious amalgamation of parts of existing sales and the sales which are to be achieved by expansion. Only very occasionally will there be units which are identical with the present sales departments or units directed solely at new sources of turnover.

DIRECTION OF EXPANSION

The first step in developing a growth policy is to determine the direction that expansion will take. At the present time, when business is subject to such dynamic and continual development that a market sometimes alters completely within a couple of years, it is essential for the development of a concern to find those market sectors which offer the biggest growth opportunities. Expansion should be directed towards these. Such a choice will demand understanding of the future, but not solely commercial understanding. The starting-point may be the market, but this is, in part, determined by those already selling in the market, their production units, their development and research plans and finally their own approach to marketing.

In making a decision, the potentialities of the group's own production and development must be taken into account. This means that considerations must also include the investment plans which, in any case, must be submitted to the group management during the first months of the merger. Choice can, in part, be rationalized with the help of reports from those who are responsible for production, sales and development. In the last instance, however, the management will have to show its mettle. It will have to detach itself from the immediate situation and take responsibility for decisions based, not only on rational factors, but especially on experience and a feeling for developments.

GROUPING CUSTOMERS AND PRODUCTS

A mathematician would call a market a two-dimensional phenomenon: there are customers, and products which are bought by them. No matter how clear the broad outline finally chosen for expansion, to realize policy it is necessary to translate this broad outline into products and customers. *Within one year after the merger— before the steps which are to produce the expansion are begun—there must be a four-or-five-year commercial plan specifying the turnovers aimed at, analysed by customers and products.* The principal ones must be mentioned by type and name, the others set out in product and consumer groups. To get an impression of the group's profitability and liquidity during the first few years, a forecast must be made for the main sub-divisions of the turnover, of the expected yield, prices, costs, the minimum quality requirements of the product and the expected conditions of payment for sales and purchasing.

Any experienced sales manager will point out that this commercial plan, will, during the course of the four or five years it covers, develop on numerous points which were not foreseen. This is true, but of course the plan is not meant to be followed blindly—even if this were possible. It is meant as an indicator and guide for the commercial units which will be created during the last phase of the merger process. In the case of sudden changes in the commercial situation, it will enable the managers of the sales units and the concern management to see at once the effect these changes will have on the entire group policy, and to adapt to these changes more quickly than the group's competitors.

HOMOGENEOUS PUBLIC RESPONSE FOR EACH GROUP

The choice of the expansion policy and the commercial long-term plan are the first two steps of the commercial policy. The third, on which the success of the expansion will finally depend, is the reconstruction of the existing sales departments into a number of new sales units, which will, together, have to make the planned expansion of the turnover a reality.

It must be realized what tremendous opportunities the merger offers. The scale-increasing merger, in contrast to vertical integration, offers a wider market for the products of each of the partners; the customers of these partners are offered a wider range of products. In the forecast expansion shown in the commercial plan, this has, of course, been taken into account. The aim is to weld the existing sales departments, which during the first year of the merger have been given greater independence (see pages 153–156) into a number of new sales units. These must be constructed in such a way that they can make optimum use of the specific opportunities offered by the merger. It was shown earlier (see pages 152–153) that the power of any sales unit, the result of all its sales efforts, is determined by the subjective image the firm assumes for its customers. The most essential characteristic which public response should have is complete homogeneity. It must be entirely free from any ambiguity, which creates uncertainty.

This homogeneity must be established in each of the new sales units, giving each a clear personality. Primarily, this personality is obtained by dividing products and customers into groups according to this idea. An increase in range—within the sales unit—may be useful, but should not be overdone. There is a limit to the products which can be covered by one sales unit; a penny product does not go well with a guinea product; plastics are at odds with steel. This also applies to customers. Supplying the retail trade will create difficulties with the wholesaler; a solid EEC position is worlds apart from a hit-and-run overseas export at mass market prices.

The analysis of products and customers on which this division into units must be based, varies extremely widely as between branches of industry and size of company. But, here also, apart from the analysis and business acumen, a wide knowledge of the market situation will be decisive.

EXTENSION OF SALES UNITS

The grouping of products and customers into homogeneous public response entities is only the blueprint for the sales units. A homogenous public response demands more. A sales policy, product policy and price policy must be planned for each of the units separately. The units must be staffed by people who fit into this policy but who will also, by their teamwork, strengthen homogeneity within the sales department. Finally, the most important point of all: the group policy behind the sales units must enhance this image of unity by proving, wherever it meets the public eye, that what is demonstrated in the sales departments is not a façade covering a totally different reality.

At this point one of the secondary advantages of a merger should be noted. It has found that now, more than was ever possible in the original company, the special aptitudes of certain executives can be used and the special shortcomings of others compensated for. At last—it might be said—there is a chance of re-organizing personnel without treading on too many toes. For many people the merger is obviously a more comprehensible and acceptable reason than any of the arguments usually put forward in reorganizations. This advantage may sometimes become so important as to become a reason for the merger, e.g. in succession problems at managing director level.

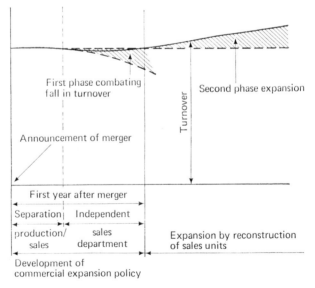

Fig. 8. Second phase of merger. After combating the fall in turnover (first phase), the expansion (second phase) starts with the new commercial policy.

If the diversity of products and customers is considerable, this requirement may have far-reaching consequences for the structure of the entire concern. It may be necessary to drop an iron curtain between a sales unit and its production basis; indeed, in some cases the integration in production and development sectors may have to be restricted by forming separate units, each connected with its own sales unit.

CONCLUSION

Our picture of the commercial policy in scale-increasing mergers is now complete. The two phases: the first building up a bulwark to prevent falling turnover, and the second heralding the expansion of the new concern, have been combined in Figure 8.

Understanding and knowledge have been crystallized into a clear plan of commercial action. The theoretical work has now been concluded and the big task facing the concern is the realization of its policy. Our studies must now be replaced by leadership, a leadership which will require the merger partners to rise to the level of a modern industrial concern, and forgetting prejudice and chauvinism, to work together for the benefit of the new concern. A human task of the highest order.

5 Human Factors

People are sometimes, justifiably, accused of paying too little attention to the human factor when dealing with mergers. Certainly, the human role in any merger process is decisive in everything that happens. Equally certain, however, is the fact that hardly any other problem is—or can be—so hard to solve as that of the human beings involved in a merger. But, so long as one has nothing else to offer than clichés or the impossible advice of the so-called conventional organization theory, there is little point in 'paying attention' to the problem. It is therefore not by chance that of the numerous aspects of the merger in this book, the human factor is dealt with last of all.

Every merger has its victims; this is apparently inevitable. Sometimes a veritable host seem to fall in the process. Although mergers and their internal consequences are not infrequently shrouded in a veil of mystery, one may assume that there are always victims. But, we must also assume that in virtually all cases special care was exercised (or at any rate that this was the intention) with regard to human problems.

One might even say that the human problem in a merger is no greater than it is without that merger. It only becomes *acute* in the case of a merger, as do so many other problems. The dismissal of a director, who, if there had not been a merger might have been able to keep his company going for a few more years, but who, after the merger soon proves himself unacceptable, cannot be used as an argument against mergers. Nor may the executives and workmen, living in the apparent security of a company which is slowly going downhill, and proving redundant after the merger, be cited as examples of careless treatment in mergers.

Mergers make everything show up more clearly, including any shortcomings in the planning and organization of a company and the people in the company which up till then had not been recognized or suspected.

Should a merger fall through, simply because it is certain that such a merger will have unpleasant consequences for directors, executives or groups of workmen? This is a question which cannot be answered, for one might think of circumstances in which postponement or even the decision not to merge would be justified for these very reasons.

But if this is not the case, the suffering caused by the merger must be mitigated as much as possible, although this does not necessarily constitute a solution to the human problems.

One of the main reasons for many problems after the merger is the fact that the executives responsible simply have not foreseen them, partly through inexperience in mergers, partly because insufficient attention had been given to certain aspects of the merger at the planning stage.

Another important factor concerns the directors/negotiators. Few things are more difficult than to place oneself (and one's own firm) in the hypothetical perspective of the future. For this one needs to be able to assess oneself impartially. Those who can do this successfully are rare indeed.

This chapter, therefore, does not offer any solution to these problems. In 'The human risks in mergers', below, a number of human risks in these circumstances are analysed, and an attempt is made to explain them and—on the basis that to be forewarned is to be forearmed—it is shown how such risks may be avoided. 'Human problems in a merger' probes more deeply into the causes of the problems of employees (including the top executives) and—taking as its starting-point the motivation of security—shows in what directions a solution might be sought.

THE HUMAN RISKS IN MERGERS

THE NEW POLICY

Within the new concern, each equal partner retains a relative voice in its affairs. A take-over means that one partner is swallowed up by the other. The heart of the problem in a merger is the fact that a new concern is created, demanding a new policy.

The word 'policy' however, means so much—and at the same time so little—that it is often used in situations where the term cannot be precisely defined, rather than in those cases where problems of policy are actually being tackled. In other words, policy is a modern escape word which—as soon as we use it— excuses us from defining exactly what we mean.

How many businessmen would be able to formulate clearly and precisely the policy they pursue in and with their own company? And, even if they are able to do so, to what extent do their words correspond with the facts applying to their company?

Of course they pursue a policy, even though they may not be particularly interested in putting it into words, for a definition has no part in the realization of that policy. The policy lies in themselves. They need only follow their intuition and their vision. This is the central problem of policy in a merger, for expansion by leaps and bounds which a merger implies, demands a *new* policy. We cannot then content ourselves with a vague new direction, intuitively understood by both parties.

It is not the words describing the integrated factory or the reorganized personnel policy, or on the common laboratory that are important, but the *definite* action plans covering all aspects of the enterprise, with their consequences for personnel and finance, *with* their sacrifices of the closing of departments, the selling of premises, problematic top executives and commercial risks, etc.

That policy, formulated and defined in a precise plan where anyone can read what successive steps will be taken once the merger has become a fact, proves to be the only way—and not even then a conclusive one—to avoid the risk of having created a company in which words may suggest an agreement, which in practice does not exist.

DETERMINING THE NEW POLICY; PRELIMINARY TALKS

In practice, during the preliminary talks the new policy is either not adequately determined or not even determined at all. This is partly, because, at this stage, the company is discussed as a whole, a totality. The negotiators are not concerned with the sales of a product or a piece of land, nor with a part of the capital or a department of the company, but with everything; practically nothing is excluded. Those concerned are therefore extremely circumspect.

Lack of familiarity with the procedure plays a part: what kind of transaction is a merger? It is neither a purchase nor a sale, although it is a bit like both. There is no clear 'supply and demand' situation. In fact, it is not even clear what the return will be and what sacrifices are required to obtain that return. In addition, motives other than business also play a part. The comparison between merger negotiations and engagements and marriages is trite, but, in part, justified. Not infrequently it is love-at-first-sight which brings the partners together, although in this case the girl must always have money! One might say that in merger negotiations love and business go hand-in-hand. Needless to say, this never helps to clarify the position.

Perhaps as a result of this situation, merger talks always have a number of characteristics in common:

1 The personal motives for the decision (or the considerations) to merge differ greatly and—which is worse—only those parts of the motives which are considered not to be dangerous to the consultations shows on the surface.

2 There is a strong inclination to pass over differences of opinion, particularly if these concern uncertain future developments. There is a wish for the talks to be agreeable. Differences of opinion are left until after the merger.

3 A common, clear over-all picture of the combined concern after the merger rarely develops. Each party has built up (with the best possible intentions) a picture of the new concern from its own situation and often has the feeling that the others will adapt themselves to this view. Naturally, these ideas differ far more widely than was apparent during the negotiations. But this too, only becomes clear after the merger.

4 Finally, there is another completely different characteristic, the consequences of which also only become apparent after the merger.

Those participating in the merger talks are always entrepreneurs, and what—perhaps a trifle exaggerated—are entrepreneurs?

1 They are almost always people in whom intuition and vision are predominant.

2   They are generally highly opinionated people, especially with
    regard to their own ideas (opinionated in the better sense of
    the word).
3   They are often somewhat dictatorial (even though today this
    dictatorship is realized more democratically).
4   They are not accustomed to discussing their decisions and taking
    into account the written and unwritten laws, traditions and
    ideas of other differently developed companies.
5   They have frequently reached an age where the chance of any
    change in their pattern of behaviour must be considered
    doubtful.

In view of all these considerations, it will be clear that there may
be a world of difference between the ideas parties have during the
preliminary talks and the reality which takes shape after the
merger contract has been signed.

THE HUMAN RISK

The difference between expectations prior to, and the reality after,
the merger, begins to show when each of the group directors, the
morning after, begins to pursue policy independently. There can be
little doubt that if their policy really proves to be contradictory,
this will be fatal for the new concern, however soundly it may have
been planned.

That such business differences often develop into personal ones
is not surprising either. In these cases, a struggle develops where no
means are left untried. The outcome is always the same: the downfall
of one of the parties concerned—or the ruin of the concern.

The reasons for this have already been mentioned. Before the
merger, words could suffice. The fact that the talks were confused
both psychologically and economically does not in itself make the
talks impossible. For no-one puts all his cards on the table during
negotiations?

Such circumstances do not impede the negotiations. Decisions
are made during the preliminary consultations in one's own company
and not with the other partner. After the merger, however, deeds
will clearly demonstrate what had always been shrouded in words.
Decisions must now be made with the others, all the cards *must* be
put on the table.

The question remains: can this risk which parties incur in any merger and which is a purely human risk, be prevented, or at any rate, reduced?

Two factors play a part. These are explained briefly below:

1 It is of the utmost importance to try to clarify and compare ideas during the negotiations; what do partners really think will be the future development of the concern? The more definite the development plan drawn up beforehand, the more the decisions are brought forward, and the smaller also will be the risk of disastrous developments.

2 Equally important, especially in strictly personal matters, is complete frankness. This presents a problem, for the position of merger talks is one of negotiation; such a position does not always allow one to be frank and outspoken. Nevertheless, it is a fact that the human risk decreases in inverse ratio to the degree of frankness. It is, however, impossible to eliminate this contradiction entirely.

In practice, however—perhaps a matter of natural protection— healthy companies succeed better in being frank than weaker firms. In other words, the human risk in a merger is decidedly smaller in a merger between healthy companies.

Perhaps this is one of the main reasons why so-called defensive mergers are so risky and are almost always doomed to fail or to be swallowed up in a larger concern. In such cases it is practically always preferable to realize co-operation by means of one or more take-overs and not by a merger. In that case the risk of a dualistic policy is avoided, for in a take-over the policy is decided beforehand. It is the—written or unwritten—policy of the acquiring company. This policy may be weak, but it is a fact that two or three different policies within a firm are more harmful than one policy, even if it is a weak one.

There is, however, in our present society a persistent feeling that it is somehow shameful to join up with a larger unit and therefore to 'be taken over'. It is something which should only be considered as a last resort. A merger shows one is 'moving with the times', while a take-over is regarded as a capitulation under the pressure of the times.

This is an error. Experience shows that companies which have been taken over, almost always prosper. It also shows that the changes brought about in healthy companies are very few and those in weak companies are often felt to be salutary.

Another aspect of the take-over is that the capital invested in a company is assured: either by payment in cash or by payment in marketable shares.

There is also the fact that, in a take-over, compensation can be demanded for redundant executives which may alleviate or eliminate any painful effects of a reorganization.

All these aspects are lacking in a merger. The birth pangs are considerable. The chance of failure is great, and greater still if either of the parties, or both, is weak. Reorganizations can only be carried through with many delays, so the capital is at a greater risk. The employees—from the directors to the workmen and women—will find themselves in an uncertain position with regard to their future. If reorganizations are necessary, they can frequently only be carried through when it is too late.

A final point in this connection is the matter of valuation. In a take-over one sells. The maximum price is determined by the value which the company has for the buyer. In a merger one contributes. The maximum value is attained by the sum—in each case determined according to the same criteria—which the company is worth in relation to the other companies. This means that—even apart from the risk that the group's capital runs in a merger—the return in a take-over is often more than the contributing value of a company in a merger.

Summing up, we arrive at the following conclusions:

1 A merger differs materially from a take-over.
2 In a merger, the heart of the problem is the formulation of the new policy.
3 A merger requires realism and frankness from the participants.
4 If partners cannot, or dare not, be frank or realistic, they should not consider a merger.
5 Sound companies can afford to be frank and realistic.
6 Weak firms have too much to hide; the chance of success is small.
7 For weak companies, a take-over is preferable to a merger.
8 There is nothing shameful in being taken over. It is frequently profitable.
9 The main problem in a take-over is the price.

THE HUMAN PROBLEMS IN A MERGER

The chief human problems in a merger are caused by the sudden increase in scale and the need for transferring existing loyalties and ties to other people, methods and purposes. It must be stressed that mergers do *not* threaten the existence of the workmen concerned, but there is a need for adequate measures with regard to retraining, transfer, and transition to shift work, as these prove necessary in many mergers. It seems common sense that changes in merged companies should be limited to those parts of the company where integration or specialization offer clear advantages. There are also obvious advantages of a plan for these alterations, a plan which is completed soon after the merger has become a fact, which clearly shows everyone's part in these changes, and carefully explains that part at all levels of organization.

MERGERS

A merger is a form of co-operation in which *all* the partners relinquish their independence, and then together proceed further to shape the purposes and the realization of the co-operation. In a merger, the first and principal task is to create a new comprehensive policy. The formal decision to merge does not contribute to such a policy. All it does is create a vacuum—space for a new policy. Filling this space with a comprehensive vision of the purposes and the way to realize these purposes—for that is what policy is—and at the same time persuading the component companies to work towards that vision, is the real merger process. Merging also means accelerated alteration, one might even call it a revolution, for a merger resembles a political revolution on a number of points:

1 Both have need of a conscious leadership with a vision, an ideal. Otherwise, it would not be possible to propel all the heterogeneous powers in one direction.
2 There is a temporary need for a stricter hierarchy; in contrast to the normal situation, many initiatives must be pushed through from a new central policy and the day-to-day work provides little direction as to what should be done.

3 Practical experiments must be carried out along fresh roads; otherwise it will take too long before there are results.
4 Conservative elements must be kept out of the top management. Under conservative leadership nothing will alter except that the independence of the partners will be lost.

Basically, a merger is a revolution which must be carefully planned:

1 Alterations and integration must be limited to those functions where the merger opens up new possibilities either commercially, technologically or in product development, and even then must be carried out only after an objective has been clearly defined.
2 The daily work in the companies must be carried on with renewed energy, particularly in places where nothing need be changed. Conservatism, in the good sense, is worth far more than a senseless urge for replacement.
3 Everything possible must be done, to repel systematically the attack of competitors which every merger seems to invite.

The merger process must be balanced. In the partner companies there are, on the one hand, sectors where renewal and integration will assure long-term growth, and on the other, sectors where hard work along the old lines will provide safety during the dangerous period just after the merger. If this balance is lacking, the merger is doomed to fail.

HUMAN PROBLEMS

Human problems are never greater than when a merger has failed, with large-scale dismissals, recriminations at the top and, worst of all, the feeling of personal failure. A successful merger, however, also affects those concerned. The basic cause of the human problems in a good merger is to be found in the differences in character and mentality of the companies and, therefore, in the differences in thought, behaviour and action of their employees. Obviously, the people concerned are generally quite unconscious of these differences. These are characteristics (ideas, dogmas, attitudes, behaviour) often developed during an existence covering several generations. They develop into indoctrination of the employees beginning at selection (in all ranks) and strengthened over the years. These differences will apply the more the nearer the employee is to the top. They are, however, just as clearly perceptible in the workmen in the factory who have been in the company's employment for a long time. The differences do not make themselves felt during the negotiations. When the strong desire to co-operate outweighs any concern with regard to concrete problems. They only become apparent later, when common decisions must actually be made.

The approach to human problems in mergers appears from this angle, to offer little that is useful—even though the existence of these differences should be acknowledged. At most, recognition of this fact can be an argument in the negotiations. In the case of widely differing characters, a merger is inadvisable. Usually this does not happen, for it is extremely difficult to define characters, let alone make any forecasts as to the chances of a successful combination. Once the merger talks have succeeded, the question arises of how the human problems emerging after the formal merger can be reduced to reasonable proportions. At this point we should stop regarding the company in a somewhat philosophical or psychological light and concentrate on the facts.

Considering a series of cases, the conclusion is that two definite causes often create great personal problems:

1 The necessity to transfer loyalties and ties.
2 The necessity to think in a new and larger whole; on a larger scale.

A merger causes great pressure on loyalties and ties with people and companies:

1 At every level but especially at the top many people will have a different chief.
2 Frequently they will have to adapt to people, matters and methods they hardly know, which break through customs of many years' standing, and which perhaps a short time ago still seemed utterly unacceptable.
3 For the sake of unity in policy employees must work for ideas which at the best only partly agree with the policies they have pursued for years, and ideas which have not yet been proved by results.

In such working conditions, many people will have a rough time: both with themselves and with their job environment. Eliminating these difficulties is impossible but they can be mitigated:

1 By a personnel policy which can best be described as honest and well-considered.
2 By a clear central policy, based on convincing ideas, precisely formulated, which is carefully communicated to all employees and executed without delay.

Scale-increase in thought is just as difficult a requirement, but the success of the merger nevertheless depends on it:

1 In the new policy the new problem of co-ordinating big independent companies must not only be solved, but completely new aspects of management will become urgent (e.g. new mechanized equipment, wage talks, an increased share in the market, price leadership, etc.): in the top management it will soon become mercilessly clear who can cope with these problems and who cannot.
2 It is difficult to keep the group as a whole in view; matters which formerly could be dealt with independently, must now be tested against overall policy. Sometimes consultation with the top management will even formally be required. The first will be hard for many employees, the second may well be disagreeable.
3 As decisions must now cover a longer distance, the preparations and the actual decision-making will have to be done more rapidly, otherwise the general trend will suffer; for some people this speed will prove impossible.
4 All the existing functions and specializations will not only demand a wider practical knowledge and at the same time greater capacity for abstract thought, but also new functions and specializations will develop from tasks which formerly comprised more but did not go so deep. In many positions employees will fail to meet these requirements; in other jobs people will have to submit to a new hierarchy within more limited bounds.
5 Many activities expand and yet receive less notice; those dealing with such activities must do more with less supervision, a change to which not all will prove equal.

It is almost inevitable that some people will prove unable to cope with the heavy demands made by the increase in scale. Several measures may, however, assist them:

1 The group policy can be translated for all employees into a series of concrete, quantified and temporized objectives.
2 These objectives can be set out as so many tasks; this will give a better result than it does to set out tasks as definite powers and responsibilities (see also pages 147–150).
3 Functions or parts of the company which have no place in the new policy, and are a nuisance because of the detailed attention they require, must unhesitatingly be abolished, farmed out, closed down or sold.

SPECIFIC PROBLEMS AT ALL LEVELS OF ORGANIZATION

If the human problems in a merger are considered not from the point of main causes, but at each level of the organization, we shall find similar problems there, and quite different ones.

At director level, not a single task will remain entirely the same. In practice, the general management policy will, sooner or later, come to rest in the hands of a group of, at the most, three people. The roundabout way of a large board of directors including all the partner directors will, de facto, lead to the same result, although often more painfully. The danger threatening the two or three top men is that they will fail in the united development or transmission of their policy. The other executive directors are faced with the difficult task of specializing in a sector or aspect of the management, and conforming to the new policy. This specialization will, however, often—at the human level as well—show surprising opportunities for development, especially because of the much larger scale on which specialization is possible in a good merger. For directors who are not capable of such growth, and who may not even share the new ideas on policy, life will become very difficult, the more so as lack of capability, particularly at top level, becomes so mercilessly apparent in a merger.

It is better to include a considerable sum under 'liabilities' on the merger balance sheet for 'honourable retirement' than at a later date to find the same or an even larger amount listed as losses on the Profit and Loss Account due to failure of the merger process. This certainly also holds good for the people concerned, especially if they are shareholders as well. Unfortunately, true wisdom in this respect is rare.

Many of the merger problems for top executives are comparable to those for directors. They are, however, not always treated with as much generosity and consideration. Those who think that the *justitia distributiva* should make way for opportunism, should remember that unwarranted hard action against weaker executives, especially in cases where directors have been shielded, will cause the real executives to have an equally 'unwarranted' interest in the employment columns in the press.

One problem which affects the executives far more than the directors in a merger is that of uncertainty. For one thing, uncertainty arises because the merger talks must necessarily be kept secret and the merger therefore comes as a surprise. This uncertainty is further strengthened by the fact that clear plans on policy take an unnecessarily long time to announce, because a number of specialist and advisory functions are duplicated.

For the entire team, rapid publication of a clear policy plan, with purposes for each function, is the best means of combating the slowness and lack of decisiveness which causes uncertainty. Just as in the case of directors, however, compromises and halfheartedness do more harm than a really generous 'golden handshake' where this is required.

For a great many executives, the merger will mean a narrowing and deepening of their work, and it is of great importance to accelerate this process by means of clear objectives, a rapid restructuring of tasks, and internal and external training.

Factory and office workers are least threatened by the merger, although facts may seem to show otherwise. Sometimes factories have been closed down as a result of mergers, but this is generally the result of weakness in respect of trend, structure or policy. In such cases, the merger is not the cause of the closure, and serves to prevent even more damaging measures. But, although the merger may not be the cause, the obligation for job security in such a situation remains the same and demands adequate and careful settlement. Most mergers are not defensive but offensive actions, causing expansion rather than reduction of employment.

In fact, the big problems for employees in a merger lie in the offensive dynamic character of a good merger. Specialization and investment in depth especially cause both a great number of internal transfers and a tendency towards shift-work. The retraining and adaptation this requires from the employees necessitates good personnel planning, increased training activities and exact regulations. Even then, there will still be many individual problems requiring careful attention.

It is, therefore, clear that, in arrangements concerning employees in a merger, special thought should be given to retraining, transfer and transition to shift-work rather than to the possible results of a closure.

MERGER OR TAKE-OVER

Much of what has been said here about mergers also applies to take-overs. In take-overs there is, however, one essential point which lends a different character to all problems including the human ones. From the first there is practically always, a clear policy which is energetically pursued—that is, the policy of the acquiring party. Moreover, there is a definite example of much that is to be introduced, for the policy of the acquiring party will, of course, have long been pursued in its own firm. The changes are no less, but almost all the uncertainty at every level is absent or lasts only for a short time. Take-overs can have the greatest advantages for all parties. So often it is, unfortunately, the defensive merger which attracts more than the offensive merger or take-over. The main reason for this lies in the chief human problem in take-overs; the transfer of independence. This is why take-overs are also called mergers.

Mergers open up immense new possibilities for the parties in both business and human terms.

The good merger will often create a new strong concern which will itself be capable of effecting take-overs within a comparatively short period.

6 Postscript—The United Kingdom and Europe

This book was originally written for Dutch businessmen based on experiences in Holland and other EEC countries. However, what was written for the benefit of Dutch companies applies with equal force to other countries, including the United Kingdom. Naturally, regulations regarding company law, taxation, inheritance, marriage settlements and stock exchange procedure, vary from country to country, and where inter-country agreements are affected these can cause problems. Nevertheless, the broad principles of merger policy outlined in this book have a more or less universal application, no matter in which country one is operating.

Although the principles the book lays down may require some modification, they are of equal, if not greater, importance for companies contemplating international expansion, and particularly for British companies thinking in terms of expansion into Europe.

Indeed, the loss of the Empire and the ending of Imperial Preference in recent years has made it imperative for many firms in the UK to strengthen their position by mergers, either at home, or in international markets. And more of these will be needed if Britain is to solve her current Balance of Payments problems. Of course, Europe does not provide the UK with a ready-made 'home' market, as it would were she a member of the EEC. Nevertheless, business is already highly international in scope, and the profitable excursions made so far into Europe by Britain's biggest industrial groupings illustrate quite clearly that the benefits are there to be reaped, if only the right efforts are made at the right time.

The development towards an enlarged home market in Europe is gathering momentum and within the EEC itself much integration and specialization is taking place. Whether or not Britain becomes a member of the Common Market in its present form remains to be seen, but even if she does not, the UK and the other EFTA countries will inevitably find that, in many fields, they are being drawn closer to an economic United States of Europe or a European home market.

Before considering international expansion, it is vital that the company should have a clear and dispassionate assessment of its development potential in its own country. Once this is done, the company can then look towards Europe. As a period of intensive research and forward-thinking is required to make an assessment of potential in European terms, it is important that companies should set about their European plans well in advance of taking the actual decision to 'go European'.

All forms of co-operation discussed in this book are open to the British company looking for a European partner, whether the need is for a full take-over, merger, co-operation on product ranges, joint venture or licensing agreements.

STEPS TO FULL INTEGRATION

Co-operation in a limited way may well be the first step to fuller integration. Flexible arrangements can be made which can easily be unscrambled if they do not work out to the satisfaction of everyone concerned. But, there are disadvantages in limited forms of co-operation. British companies should also remember that, in many continental countries, requirements on disclosure of company affairs and finances are far less stringent than in the UK and many companies are reluctant to exchange vital information, even with companies with whom they may be considering an agreement of one form or another.

This is only one of the reasons why a true merger is rarely the right form of co-operation between companies in different countries. For a merger to work out, the full agreement and collaboration of two approximately equal partners is necessary. It is fraught with problems and takes at least a year to achieve. When different countries are involved, the complications multiply and only in ideal circumstances will a true merger be possible, given the best possible will on both sides. Even so, the analysis of mergers will repay study by those seeking opportunities for take-over, or who may themselves wish to be acquired.

Given that European expansion is desirable, the take-over by the larger company of the smaller is usually the best form of full co-operation to adopt. British business has an immense store of experience in the international trading and financial and management spheres, which can be of inestimable value to Europe as a whole, where, generally speaking, companies are far more fragmented and far more family-controlled than in the UK. This factor, when tactfully put across, is readily appreciated by many continental business people, provided the patronizing approach is avoided.

There are, therefore, immense advantages for the UK company in acquiring continental subsidiaries which may offer a ready made entrée into the European market with a product already accepted in the European market.

Before any business venture into European countries is considered, it is vital that the UK executives first realize that other countries' business methods are very different in material respects to the British, and also that if they are to do business with European nationals they must understand their ways and seek to do business in Europe in a European manner rather than to impose British ways of life and characteristics upon the Continental.

The different structure of the business community in each country must also be carefully analysed and understood. For example, in Holland there are no exact parallels to the UK merchant banks. The *directeur* is very different to the English director, of whom the true equivalent is normally known as a manager. Such differences proliferate, and unless a clear understanding of these is made before any form of negotiation or co-operation commences, mis-understandings will follow which will undermine the agreement.

It is well known, for example, that the attitude towards the tax authorities in, say, Italy is very different from that of UK business-men to the Inland Revenue. Whereas all businessmen wish to pay as little tax as possible, the tactics which prove most successful in minimizing tax liabilities are very different. A UK businessman who attempted to settle his tax matters in Italy as he would in the UK would almost certainly find himself paying an excessive amount.

Equally, it is no use a UK company trying to force upon a European a product which simply does not cater for the European's requirements having regard to his personal environment. This may appear to be very obvious—but how often is it ignored.

Generally, only by utilizing good local management can European companies be effectively managed and developed. This is not to say that UK and other companies' management have nothing to offer to the management of European companies. They have, and as a partnership with local European management form a very strong combination. If this point is accepted, one fundamental requirement of any European company to be acquired by a company from another country, is that the European company has itself good management.

Nothing that has been said implies that the acquiring company should not take real formal control and policy direction. The execution of those policies should be by a management well versed in the environment of the country concerned. Occasionally, foreign management can be brought into a continental company. In those relatively few cases where this can be done successfully it is absolutely essential, for example, that the new management can speak fluently the language of the country and district concerned. Without this, understanding and human relations will be superficial.

Training of local management, and experience gained by them with the parent company or other companies within an international or European group, will be of inestimable value, but this, in itself, does not depart from the principle that local management of companies is best.

Where advice is needed on the management structure, legal, taxation, and financial matters, it should be taken from local firms, or from those who really are experienced in the particular locality. There are few really qualified international advisers who are competent to do this without the support of local advisers. Practices for the valuation of companies vary substantially from country to country and it is vital that advisers who are thoroughly familiar in detail with the methods adopted in a country should be consulted.

Again, the organization of professional advisers is very different from country to country and, as with the human approach, a precise assessment of the matters covered by the various professions must be made before approaches are made to them. Different business methods will require different forms of advice as between one country and another. In addition, professional standards differ substantially from country to country. The extremes of good and bad within a profession vary, and before any approach is made to any professional for specific advice, an introduction must be obtained on a thoroughly reputable and well-informed level.

For the UK company going international or European, there will be certain technical matters to satisfy and plan within exchange control, taxation, and other legislation, and, of course, companies will be adequately advised by their UK professional advisers.

In conclusion, we would say that, although there are many pitfalls for the British company going in to Europe, the opportunities are there—and they are immense. The right approach and a willingness to operate in a foreign market in accordance with the business methods of that market can bring substantial rewards.

Index